OR
SEVEN INCREASINGLY EVENTFUL YEARS
AT A CERTAIN SCHOOL OF MAGIC AND MAGIC
One Act Edition

By Matt Cox

With Additional Material Contributed by
Kristin McCarthy Parker, Stephen Stout, and Colin Waitt

Extra Zach Smith Materials by Nick Carrillo

PUFFS, OR: SEVEN INCREASINGLY EVENTFUL YEARS AT A CERTAIN SCHOOL OF MAGIC AND MAGIC
Copyright © 2018, Matt Cox
All Rights Reserved
ISBN: 9781729310359

For everyone never destined to save the world.

...Also, Mom & Dad. Them too.

Foreword from the Author

What better way to begin than an overly excited, elongated greeting: Hiiiiiii!

Welcome to the script for *Puffs, Or: Seven Increasingly Eventful Years at a Certain School of Magic and Magic*. A play which never anticipated existing in your hands as it currently is. (Digitally, physically, metaphorically, wherever we are technology-wise when you are reading this.) Thanks for buying it! This little wizard show was originally supposed to run for five performances at The Peoples Improv Theater in NYC and be done. There was a hope that maybe some friends, or the elusive non-friend, would come and see it, and there was an even more outlandish hope that perhaps those friends and non-friends would enjoy themselves. Many years later, at the time of this writing at least, *Puffs* has been running Off-Broadway for more than 600 performances, with another full year on sale. It ran for several months and broke records in Melbourne, Australia. It was filmed and screened in movie theaters nationwide. All of that with hopes for even more exciting things to come. I can't speak to what has happened since, whenever it is that you may be reading this, but I'm sure something somewhere can tell you, and who knows, maybe it's good news. It might also not be. And if that is the case, well. It's fine.

All of that is to say, this thing with words on it you hold is a culmination of lots of love, care, friendship, and oh-so-much work by an increasingly large number of humans, artists, and audiences who have willed this thing to continue to exist until it reached you. It is, dare I say (I dare), proof that magic is real, in some form at least. We discovered it, and somehow managed to put it here amongst these sentences. Maybe you can find it.

For anyone new joining us, *Puffs* is, in fact, a play. (Surprise?) Meaning, the text that follows will be broken down into lines of dialogue and stage direction, and unless something terrible has happened, a story will emerge. With the hope that there may be some of you out there who just would like to experience this thing via the page (hiii!), I have attempted to make this script a bit more fun for just reading. Those of you who have found yourselves involved in your own performance of *Puffs*, well, welcome to the family.

This script does contain some differences as to what you may find in your average play text. There's some reason for that—and good news, I'll tell you why. For many months of *Puffs'* original run, I also ran the sound from my computer atop a small ledge. *(There are many sound cues, and I will apologize now to any future designers in charge of this.)* Due to this, I was at every show for the first few months. Couple that with I, as an actor before a writer, generally try to write things that are ultimately fun to *be* in, to *play in.* Given we were at an improv theater, we had the opportunity to really play with the script over time in performance. This adds some fun oddities, and I hope you will enjoy getting to peek behind the curtain of where these bits are. For those performing the show—there are parts of this script where anyone performing in it is encouraged to make something else up. Have some fun, and please be funny, as it ultimately reflects upon me. There are other parts where there are multiple versions of the dialogue the actors may choose night to night. Please, switch it up. Let it be fun for everyone to have some variety. Don't tell the others what you are doing. It's a good time. There are even multiple versions of the script itself—the original one act version and a slightly extended two-act edition, which was created for the play in Australia, which has a few additional scenes. Then there's a version of each with a bit less language frowned upon by many parents. You can *collect 'em all, but also no pressure.*

Lastly, for those taking up the task of putting *Puffs* on, some words of *wizdom. I recommend talking fast.* You will find an early line which says the play is, depending on version, 90-ish or 110-ish minutes long. This is something of a challenge. The "-ish" affords you 10 or 15 minutes extra, but we have learned this script can easily find itself being much longer and no one wants that. So. *Talk fast.* And have fun. Too much of it. Along with that, at the back of this book you can find a glossary of phrases we like to use when talking about *Puffs.* You may or may not know it shares some similarities to another franchise *(I am of course referring to the "Rocky" films),* but we like to think of it as simply *Puffs.* Its own puff-y world, with its own puff-y words. And! The *improvised* moments—I do ask that you keep those to the places where noted. Also, no worries if you don't want to try and come up with new things—feel free to just use what's here.

Stay tuned for some more fancy extras after the script as well. We'll give you a peek behind the curtain of the show's development with some early scenes from the show's history to see how much it changed. There's also some extra Zach Smiths for your own reading enjoyment and/or horror.

This script could never have existed without the many actors who let me try out every possible phrasing and far too many new bits over the course of the show's history. I am forever in their debt. I am also in debt to the show's director, Kristin McCarthy Parker, for making a bunch of adults running around a stage in capes a wonderful experience for all; to Madeleine Bundy, who created what our Puff world looks like; and to Brian Hoes, who composed the original score. While I'm at it, more debt is owed to the incredible and loving audiences we've had over the years who have spread the word far and wide, brought large groups, written articles, or even seen us over twenty times (TWENTY TIMES!). Thanks to all of them, our producers for bringing the show to the world, all of our designers, stage managers, crew members, anyone who ever worked at the door or in the house, the parents who've seen the show an equally impressive amount of times, and really just everyone for supporting this little wizard show with some '90's jokes made by friends.

—Matt Cox

PUFFS, OR: SEVEN INCREASINGLY EVENTFUL YEARS AT A CERTAIN SCHOOL OF MAGIC AND MAGIC received its world premiere at The Peoples Improv Theater (Ali Reza Farahnakian, Founder and Caretaker; Kevin Laibson, Artistic Director) in New York City on December 5th, 2015. The producers were Stephen Stout and Colin Waitt. It was directed by Kristin McCarthy Parker; the scenic and prop design was by Liz Blessing and Madeleine Bundy; the costume design was by Madeleine Bundy; the lighting designer and production stage manager was Michelle Kelleher; the sound design was by Matt Cox; original music was by Brian Hoes. The cast was as follows:

OLIVER...Langston Belton
SUSIE/OTHERS...Madeleine Bundy
SALLY/OTHERS...Jessie Cannizzaro
J. FINCH/OTHERS...Nick Carrillo
NARRATOR...A.J. Ditty
MEGAN...Julie Ann Earls
CEDRIC/OTHERS...Evan Maltby
LEANNE/OTHERS...Andy Miller
WAYNE...Zac Moon
HANNAH/OTHERS...Eleanor Philips
ERNIE MAC/OTHERS...Stephen Stout

The play received a developmental production at The University of Florida, School of Theatre and Dance (Jerry Dickey, School Director; Jenny Goelz, Production Manager), opening June 2nd, 2016. It was presented by special arrangement with Tilted Windmills Theatricals (John Arthur Pinckard and David Carpenter). The director was Kristin McCarthy Parker; production designers were Madeleine Bundy and Liz Blessing; the scenic design was by Mihai Ciupe; props were designed by John Schluter; the lighting design was by Joseph Hodge; the costume design was by Amanda Moore; the sound design was by Matt Cox; original music was by Brian Hoes; the violence director/movement consultant was Tiza Garland; the production stage manager was Logan Vonada. The cast was as follows:

OLIVER...William Vonada
SUSIE/OTHERS...Hope Golds
SALLY/OTHERS...Asia Zaffere
J. FINCH/OTHERS...Diego Zozaya
NARRATOR...Kristina Johnson
MEGAN...Kacey Musson
CEDRIC/OTHERS...Chaz May
LEANNE/OTHERS...Nicole Cannon
WAYNE...Nick Chinaris
HANNAH/OTHERS...Marissa Toogood
ERNIE MAC/OTHERS...Ernest Briggs

PUFFS was subsequently produced Off-Broadway at The Elektra Theater, opening October 20th, 2016. It was produced by Tilted Windmills Theatricals (John Arthur Pinckard and David Carpenter), Stamatios Tom Hiotis, John Paterakis, George Stephanopoulos, Letter Blue Entertainment; in association with GG Entertainment, Invisible Wall Productions, Eric Kelhoffer, and Stephen Stout & Colin Waitt. It was directed by Kristin McCarthy Parker; the scenic and prop design was by Liz Blessing and Madeleine Bundy; the costume design was by Madeleine Bundy; the lighting design was by Michelle Kelleher; the sound design was by Matt Cox; original music was by Brian Hoes; the production stage manager was Jo Goforth. The cast was as follows:

OLIVER...Langston Belton
SUSIE/OTHERS...Madeleine Bundy
SALLY/OTHERS...Jessie Cannizzaro
J. FINCH/OTHERS...Nick Carrillo
NARRATOR...A.J. Ditty
MEGAN...Julie Ann Earls
CEDRIC/OTHERS...James Fouhey
LEANNE/OTHERS...Andy Miller
WAYNE...Zac Moon
HANNAH/OTHERS...Eleanor Philips
ERNIE MAC/OTHERS...Stephen Stout
SWING...Anna Dart
SWING...Jake Keefe

It transferred with the same cast to New World Stages, Stage 5, opening July 17th, 2017. It was produced by Tilted Windmills Theatricals (John Arthur Pinckard and David Carpenter), Stamatios Tom Hiotis, John Paterakis, George Stephanopoulos, Invisible Wall Productions, Letter Blue Entertainment, Sally Cade Holmes, Heather Shields, John Albert Harris, and Alan Koolik/David Treatman; in association with GG Entertainment, Mark & Alison Law, Paul C. Bongiorno, Oliver Baer, Eric Kelhoffer, and Stephen Stout & Colin Waitt. It was directed by Kristin McCarthy Parker; the set, costumes, and prop designer was Madeleine Bundy; the lighting design was by Herrick Goldman; the sound design was by Matt Cox; original music was by Brian Hoes; the production stage manager was Kaila Hill.

CHARACTERS

WAYNE HOPKINS
OLIVER RIVERS
MEGAN JONES
NARRATOR
ERNIE MAC and A VERY TALL MAN / SEAMUS / A CERTAIN
      POTIONS TEACHER / PROFESSOR TURBAN / GHOST
      HISTORY TEACH / PROFESSOR LOCKY / MR. NICK / SAL /
      SECOND HEADMASTER / REAL MR. MOODY
HANNAH and FIRST HEADMASTER / PROFESSOR McG /
      PROFESSOR SPROUTTY / XAVIA JONES / PROFESSOR
      LANNY / RUNES TEACH / MS. BABBLE
J. FINCH FLETCHLEY and UNCLE DAVE / GOYLE / A FAT FRIAR /
      CLUMSY LONGBOTTOM / HERMEOONE #3 / VIKTOR / MR.
      BAGMAN / ZACH SMITH
LEANNE and GINNY / HELGA / FRENCHY
SALLY PERKS and HERMEOONE / BLONDO MALFOY / ROWENA /
      RITA SCOOTER / BIPPY
SUSIE BONES and HARRY / COLIN / HERMEOONE #2 / RIC GRYFF /
      MYRTLE
CEDRIC and MR. VOLDY

DEATH BUDDIES to be played by all.

NOTES

*: Denotes two characters speak at the same time.

**: Denotes an actor may say whatever they'd like. As long as it's, you
know, funny. And makes sense. Feel free to just use what is printed here if
that is something you are not comfortable with.

***: Can change to reference the region the show is being performed in, or
a specific prop, etc.

Prologue

With little to no fanfare, a Narrator enters. They hold up a device that can turn lights off. They point the device at the lights around the theater, and each turns off one by one until...blackout.

Lights come up on that same Narrator from just a moment ago, remember them? They're now ready to tell a story. They, like many in this play, speak with a British accent, or at least an attempt at one. They are a real scholarly type and are, at their core, a Puff.

A light piano theme plays. Not the one you are hearing in your head. It's a different one. The Narrator speaks to us.

NARRATOR: Heroes. Made. Not born. Except, sometimes...they *are* born. On a gloomy night, in a far away, magical land called: England.

(Behind them A Very Tall Man with a big beard and some goggles appears holding a very, very special baby. The First Headmaster, old, kind, and gentle, enters with him. They admire this heroic, special, really, really important baby boy. The Narrator spots them.)

NARRATOR: Ah! A giant! Aw, a baby. His parents: dead. But he lives. He is *the boy who lives.* He has a *scar*. On his *forehead*. Shaped like...*you know.* You get it? You are familiar with this boy? Well. Forget about him.
A VERY TALL MAN: *Okay.
FIRST HEADMASTER: *Goodbye!

(They swiftly exit with that important baby.)

NARRATOR: This story is not about *him.*

(From seemingly nowhere, another baby appears carried by someone far less impressive, with somewhere far better to be.)

NARRATOR: Ah! Another orphan. His parents: also dead. Killed in a freak chocolate frog accident. *Please, don't ask.* This boy is whisked away to live with his uncle in the even more magical land of Cattlepoke Springs, New Mexico.

(Uncle Dave appears, beer in hand, excited for his life.)

1

UNCLE DAVE: Yee-haw!

(He is handed the baby. His joy ceases.)

UNCLE DAVE: Aw. Fuuuuuuuuuuu—
NARRATOR: Where...the boy grows up!

> *(Through the power of magic, the baby grows up into eleven-year-old Wayne Hopkins. He is playing a classic Nintendo Gameboy. Uncle Dave finishes his eleven-year-long expletive.)*

UNCLE DAVE: —uuuuuck!

(Uncle Dave pats him on the shoulder and exits.)

NARRATOR: And up until a few weeks ago, this now eleven-year-old boy had only the regular problems of a child in 1991.
WAYNE HOPKINS: Aw, man.

> *(Wayne takes the game cartridge out of the Gameboy and blows into it. An owl flies overhead screeching. Is it a real owl? Is it something representing an owl? You decide. It drops a letter to the ground. Wayne picks it up and begins to read.)*

WAYNE HOPKINS: Um...Uncle Dave? A bird flew into our living room and dropped a piece of paper that says *I'm a wizard and I need to go to school in England?!*
UNCLE DAVE (O.S.): ...What kinda bird?
WAYNE HOPKINS: An owl, I think?

(Uncle Dave enters in a hurry, zipping up his pants.)

UNCLE DAVE: Oh my Gawd! I forgot to tell you. Yer a Wizard, Wayne! ...Also, wizards exist! ...And you are one. Just like yer British parents. Oh shit! *Yer parents were British!* Wow. We gotta talk more. Come on, I'll drive ya to the airport!
NARRATOR: And before he knew it, after a confusing train station experience...

> *(Numbered train platform signs appear. A "nine" and a "ten" should do. Wayne looks confused as to what to do next. He eventually makes his way through the wall, or alternatively runs*

headfirst into it. He then makes his way to magic school, however you might like to visualize or imagine that.)

NARRATOR: Wayne found himself at the gates of a certain school of female magic and male magic. Where he would spend the next seven years. Tonight! We will be taking an incredibly in-depth look at those seven years. Over the next five hours split into two parts—

(Lights come up around the theater. The Narrator looks towards the technical booth in a slight moment of panic.)

NARRATOR: *What?!* 90-ish minutes? Oh.

(Lights return to normal.)

NARRATOR: Tonight! We will take...*a* look at those seven years. Seven years that were, in one word, eventful. It begins as these stories tend to begin...WITH A SORTING!

(The stage is full of eleven-year-old children, each waiting for their name to be called. Professor McG reads from a parchment of names, a stool in front of her. On that stool: a hat. A very important hat. A hat that will literally determine nearly every aspect of the next seven years of these poor eleven-year-olds' lives.)

PROFESSOR McG: Finnigan, Seamus!

(A student sits on the stool. The hat goes on his head. We hear a most booming and pre-recorded voice.)

SORTER HAT (V.O.): BRAVE!

(Applause as the student is given a "Brave" item.)

PROFESSOR McG: Goldstein, Anthony!

(A student sits on the stool.)

SORTER HAT (V.O.): SMART!

(The student is given a "Smart" item.)

PROFESSOR McG: It, well, it just says Goyle.
GOYLE: Goyle.

(A not so bright boy sits on the stool. The hat IMMEDIATELY sorts him.)

SORTER HAT (V.O.): SNAKE!

(This rather mean student is given a "Snake" item. Applause, but not quite as loud of applause. McG finds a name on her list that she is not quite sure how to pronounce.)

PROFESSOR McG: Um. Granger, Her... Her-mee-oh-nay?

(We focus over to Wayne talking to an unidentified student in line with him. We eventually learn this is Harry, the greatest boy who ever happened to live.)

WAYNE HOPKINS: Question. Hypothetical. What if I don't have enough of a personality for the magic talking hat to sort me? Like...how much authority does this hat really have? Never mind. ...This place is crazy huh? I never thought I'd go to school in a castle. Pretty cool. I've never really liked school. People were mean. To me. I'm talking too much. You probably have all your own nervous thoughts going on... Can I tell you something? I think I might be...special? I watch a lot of movies and read lots of books, and it's like: a *normal boy finds out he actually has amazing abilities and is swept away to a new, magical world?* Does that sound familiar? Because that is now my ACTUAL life. And THAT kid, through some incredible circumstances always becomes like *the* most important person. Like in the whole world. A sort of...Chosen One. AHH! Magic is real, and this orphaned boy wizard is ready for seven years of amazing adventures!
PROFESSOR McG: Eh. HEM! Mr. Potter!
HARRY: Oh! Excuse me.

(Harry unveils himself and brushes past Wayne. Whispers and chatter from the other students. He walks over to the stool.)

HARRY: Ohhh! No, hat! Not that! Anything but that! Please?!
SORTER HAT (V.O.): BRAVE!

(The students applaud and exit to become best friends, forever. All except Wayne, who stands unsorted. Professor McG notices him.)

PROFESSOR McG: Oh. Look. It's...another one. Um...uh. Student?
WAYNE HOPKINS: Wayne Hopkins.
PROFESSOR McG: ...Sure. Come on then.

(She waves him over. Wayne takes a few sheepish steps forward and sits on the stool. Finally, the hat booms.)

SORTER HAT (V.O.): PUFF!

(Wayne is handed a "Puff" item. Goyle pops his head out.)

GOYLE: Boooooo!

(The Narrator leaves Wayne at the stool as all exit around him. The Narrator pulls out a book with a big number 1 on it.)

NARRATOR: The Puffs. Spoiler alert: not everyone's favorite. But when a hat speaks, you listen, and the new recruits were quickly whisked away to a quaint little basement somewhere near the kitchens. Welcome! To what I like to call, YEAR ONE: THE PUFFS AND THE SORCERER'S ATTEMPT AT EARNING POINTS AND MAKING FRIENDS.

Scene: Welcome to the Puffs

Just like that we've arrived in the Puff common room, a cozy basement somewhere near the kitchens. The Puffs have all entered and stand smiling at each other. Eventually...a very excited Puff speaks.

LEANNE: Guys. Guess what? WE'RE ALL WIZARDS.

(Leanne celebrates this fact. Everyone else is not quite sure what to do.)

PUFFS: Yeah.
J. FINCH: Hey, we should all introduce ourselves! I'm J. Finch Fletchley. I'm boyish and fun.
PUFFS: HI!

(As if compelled by a higher power or something carnal within themselves, the Puffs all realize they responded the same way: a very loud "Hi." Rather than fear this, they embrace it.)

SUSIE BONES: I'm Susie Bones. Once upon a time my entire family was murdered. Except my aunt.

PUFFS: HI!

WAYNE HOPKINS: I'm Wayne. I've read *The Silmarillion*, twice.

PUFFS: HI!

SALLY PERKS: I'm Sally Perks. And I go to this school!

PUFFS: HI!

ERNIE MAC: Who's THAT?! It's me, ERNIE MAC! I'm basically the best...so. Hi.

PUFFS: HI!

HANNAH: ...Who's THAT? It's...me. Hannah. I'm Hannah.

PUFFS: HI!

LEANNE: I was raised in a cabin by my grandparents and you're the first other children I've ever seen, oh *and I'm a wizard.* And my name is Leanne.

PUFFS: HI?

*(Oliver Rivers, as will soon be discussed, does not have a British accent. He speaks with an ***American accent.)*

OLIVER RIVERS: Um, Oliver Rivers, and I'm just here to keep my head down and get a fundamental understanding of wizard-ing basics.

PUFFS: HI!

*(From the corner of the room, Megan Jones steps forward. Megan is dressed a little darker than the others, a little what one might call "goth." She does not believe she belongs in this room, nor does she want to be amongst these weirdos. But for one moment, she tries to be friendly. Like Wayne and Oliver, she speaks with an ***American accent.)*

MEGAN JONES: Um. Megan Jones.

(Many of the Puffs leap back in fear with a unified gasp. They know this name. They know what she just might be capable of. Megan decides friendliness is not worth it.)

MEGAN JONES: Yep. That's right. Just so we're clear. I'm not like you. Any of you. So. Leave me alone.

WAYNE HOPKINS: H...

PUFFS: Shhhh!

(Suddenly, descending like an angel from an unexpected place—perhaps the audience—a very cool young man enters.)

CEDRIC: And my name...is *Cedric.*

(Blaring guitars, drums, and rock concert lighting greet Cedric as he in turn greets everyone, audience included. Some Puffs applaud. Some become overwhelmed. Some have no idea what's going on but hey, they are happy to be here. Cedric eventually makes his way to the center of this clump of Puffs.)

CEDRIC: Thanks. Now, gather round. Don't be shy. Welcome to the Puffs!

CEDRIC & PUFFS TOGETHER: HI!

CEDRIC: Just a few things to get you acquainted to the school. First, the stairs move.

(Sally Perks gasps.)

CEDRIC: Don't freak out. Just breathe. Second...the Puffs don't exactly have the best reputation here. People will make jokes about you.

PUFFS: Aw.

CEDRIC: Or throw food at you.

PUFFS: Awhhh.

CEDRIC: Or they might curse you.

PUFFS: AHHHH!

CEDRIC: In fact, here is a list of curses you can expect to be hit by at some point in the next week.

(A piece of parchment, frightening in length, falls from the ceiling. Some truly terrifying and embarrassing sounding spells are listed. "Wedgi-o," "Nose-us Boogerus," "Forgetus Your Parents," etc. Spells that really make you wonder if this whole magic thing is a good idea. The Puffs all become very nervous about this terrifying place.)

CEDRIC: But, none of that matters. Because really, we're a bunch of nice, fun, happy people. Also, *badgers.* Badgers are great! That being said, there's something very important we need to discuss. What do you think the most important part of magic school is?

OLIVER RIVERS: Learning magic?

CEDRIC: Wrong.

(This marks the first time Oliver Rivers ever failed to answer a question correctly in a school.)

CEDRIC: The House Cup. Here, you earn points for doing something right, and you lose them for doing something wrong. The Puffs have come in last place in the House Cup for...ever. But together we are going to change that. This year, we're going to win. Or, we're going to get second. OR, *we're going to get third.* Third or nothing!

(Somehow, third sounds like the most enticing of the three. Cedric puts his hand out in the center and motions for the other Puffs to join him. All chant.)

PUFFS: Third or nothing. *Third or nothing!* THIRD OR NOTHING!!!!

CEDRIC: Whoever wins the most points? They'd be a real hero.

(Cedric looks to Wayne.)

WAYNE HOPKINS: *Me?*

CEDRIC: Maybe! Well, I'm off to bed.

J. FINCH: If Cedric's going to bed, I'm going to bed too! J. Finch out!

PUFFS: *Ooo! Bed! *Sleep! *I brought my own pillow! *I hope I have dreams! *Etc!

(The Puffs exit, except for Wayne, Megan, and Oliver.)

MEGAN JONES: So, it's official. The next seven years are gonna suck. Can you believe this group of dingbats?

WAYNE HOPKINS: I think everyone seems nice.

MEGAN JONES: You're talking to me? You're not running away?

OLIVER RIVERS: Why would we do that?

MEGAN JONES: Um. Everyone knows my mom worked for...*You-Know-Who.*

WAYNE & OLIVER: Who?

MEGAN JONES: *The Dark Lord.*

WAYNE & OLIVER: ...*Who?*

MEGAN JONES: Whatever, the guy was a super evil wizard.

WAYNE & OLIVER: There are *evil* wizards?!

MEGAN JONES: Yep. And my mom was one of his most feared followers. I warn you...I'm just as bad-ass as her.

(Leanne runs in.)

LEANNE: Megan! Our beds are stacked on top of each other. MAGICALLY!
MEGAN JONES: ...It's a bunk bed?

(Leanne looks to her hands in disbelief.)

LEANNE: We're wizards!

(Leanne exits.)

MEGAN JONES: Ugh. I'm going to hang out with the Snakes. *Where I belong!*
WAYNE HOPKINS: You can't leave, you might lose points.
MEGAN JONES: Watch me!

(Megan exits. A sound effect indicates that points are lost. Wayne turns to Oliver.)

WAYNE HOPKINS: So. You new to all of this too?
OLIVER RIVERS: Yep. All of it.
WAYNE HOPKINS: You're...not British!
OLIVER RIVERS: Nope. ***New Jersey.

(Note: Oliver should be from any nearby major city or place that everyone agrees kind of sucks. If you don't have such a place, New Jersey should always work. My apologies to the people of New Jersey. I truly mean nothing personal and I know dozens of great New Jersey-ians.)

OLIVER RIVERS: My family just moved to England back in May, so they'd be closer to me when I started at the Mathematical Institute at Oxford this semester.
WAYNE HOPKINS: But you're eleven.
OLIVER RIVERS: Oh, I know. I've sort of been called a "math savant." But that's not important now. Now, I'm just a wizard...a beginner level wizard. You don't think ending up here means we're already bad at wizard-ing right? I'm not used to being bad at school.

WAYNE HOPKINS: We just have to focus on earning those points and the rest will take care of itself. I mean it's just magic. How hard can it possibly be?

Scene: Studies

A bell rings. We're in a classroom now. The Puffs all rush on chatting with each other and surround Oliver and Wayne.

PUFFS: *Wow! *Class! *I brought a quill! *I brought a book! *Etc.

(A Certain Greasy Haired Potions Teacher enters.)

A CERTAIN POTIONS TEACHER: Sit. Everyone. Now. You are here to learn the art of potion ma—*Ohhhh.* Puffs.
PUFFS: Hi!
A CERTAIN POTIONS TEACHER: *(A sigh.)* Can anyone tell me... What. Is. A. Potion?

(J. Finch raises his hand.)

J. FINCH: OOO! It's what you put on your skin to make it feel soft.
A CERTAIN POTIONS TEACHER: No. That's lotion.

(Sally raises her hand.)

SALLY PERKS: It's the place all the fishes live!
A CERTAIN POTIONS TEACHER: Wrong. That's the ocean.

(Leanne raises her hand...and then you have some OPTIONS.

**The following line is anything that makes sense within the rhythm and rhyme of the bit. Below are some options. Choose one or find some of your own. After ONE of these, Oliver raises his hand.)*

LEANNE: (OPTION 1) It's a starchy root vegetable!
A CERTAIN POTIONS TEACHER: That's…a Po-tato.

LEANNE: (OPTION 2) It's the head of the Catholic Church!
A CERTAIN POTIONS TEACHER: That's…the Po-pe.

LEANNE: (OPTION 3) It's that dance where everyone is a train! Choo choo!
A CERTAIN POTIONS TEACHER: That's...the loco-motion.

LEANNE: (OPTION 4) It's the water that surrounds all the continents!
A CERTAIN POTIONS TEACHER: That is still the Ocean...

LEANNE: (OPTION 5) It's that stuff that smells good!
A CERTAIN POTIONS TEACHER: That's...Po-tpourri.

OLIVER RIVERS: It. Is. Uh. Magic liquid!
A CERTAIN POTIONS TEACHER: You are the most dunderheaded student I
    have ever seen sit in my class. If you manage to succeed in my
    course this year, I will eat a shoe. Ten points from the Puffs.
LEANNE: I ate a shoe once. It didn't taste good but it didn't taste bad.
A CERTAIN POTIONS TEACHER: ...Class dismissed.

*(A Certain Potions Teacher grumbles and leaves. A bell rings.
Professor McG enters.)*

PROFESSOR McG: Transfiguration: the art of—oh. Puffs.
PUFFS: Hi!
PROFESSOR McG: Yes, hello. Um. We're going to turn *things*. Into *other*
    things. Wooow! Go crazy.
PUFFS: YEAH! WOO!

*(Everyone starts waving their wands. Professor McG goes over to
Oliver.)*

PROFESSOR McG: Mr. Rivers. Oh dear, oh dear. Your wand technique is all
    wrong. Here, you get to use the *training wand. Oooo!* Eh hem. Five
    points from the Puffs.

*(Professor McG hands him a large and very special wand: the
Training Wand. She pats him on the head and exits. A bell rings.
Professor Turban enters wearing a turban.)*

PROFESSOR TURBAN: D...D...D...D...D...Defense! A...A...A...Against!

*(Megan Jones shoots a spitball at the back of Professor Turban's
turban. He spins around, and on the back of his turban we see a pair
of red glowing eyes staring at us. We hear a whispery voice.)*

MISTER VOLDY (V.O.): YAH! You will pay for this insolence!

(Professor Turban spins back around, embarrassed.)

OLIVER RIVERS: Uh—where did that voice come from?!
PROFESSOR TURBAN: Ten points from the P-P-Puffs!

(Professor Turban exits. The Puffs all stand frustrated at their lack of points. Points, the most important thing there will ever be.)

OLIVER RIVERS: Is there a math class? Please tell me next is math class.
WAYNE HOPKINS: We have something called...Herbology?
J. FINCH: I hope it's not scary or confusing.

(Professor Sproutty enters.)

PROFESSOR SPROUTTY: Class! We're going to look at plants!
PUFFS: YAY! PLANTS!

(Puffs and Professor Sproutty all exit, happy to go see some plants. Wayne and Oliver hang back.)

WAYNE HOPKINS: Okay. I will admit with the exception of Herbology, which is awesome, this isn't easy.
OLIVER RIVERS: Maybe we should just go sit in our room and hide for seven years so we don't lose any more points?
WAYNE HOPKINS: Come on. It's just the first day. And next we have our first flying lesson. We're right after the Braves who are...going...now?

(They look to see Harry and Blondo riding broomsticks.)

BLONDO MALFOY: If you want it so bad, you'll have to catch it!

(Blondo throws a sphere. Harry catches it. Much applause for Harry.)

HARRY: I did it. I caught the ball sphere. I did it!

(Harry exits. Blondo walks over to where Wayne and Oliver stand.)

BLONDO MALFOY: Potter. What a bluthering whimpersnatch. What are you two broom-heads looking at? EAT SLUGS!

(Blondo points his wand at Wayne and Oliver with the cruelty only an eleven-year-old can have. The two vomit slugs. Professor Sproutty enters and sees these two boys vomiting slugs.)

PROFESSOR SPROUTTY: Students vomiting slugs? What would the plants say? Fifty points from the Puffs.

BLONDO MALFOY: Ha! You've just been Malfoy-ed.

(Blondo laughs. O! What fun bullying is. Megan has entered and tried to laugh with him, but he scoffs and leaves her behind. She exits elsewhere.)

WAYNE HOPKINS: Gah! Wizard school is just like regular school!

(Wayne and Oliver exit, more slugs sure to come. The Narrator steps out with a plastic bag to remove the slugs and continue the story.)

NARRATOR: Oh, sad. Maybe it's time for something a bit more festive!

Scene: The Feast!

At the snap of the Narrator's fingers—a song that sounds something like an off-brand version of the "Monster Mash" plays. Let's call it the "Monster Bash." J. Finch runs on with other students. All wear various Halloween costumes.

J. FINCH: OOO! It's the Halloween feast! J. Finch approved!

(The Puffs form a small clump together. They dance. They chat. Megan stands apart from the group. Wayne enters. He tries to say "Hi" to Megan, but she storms off. He tries to join the group of Puffs, but they don't make room for him. He stands by himself for a moment until Oliver enters.)

WAYNE HOPKINS: Oliver! Where have you been?

OLIVER RIVERS: Sorry. I've been working on charms. I think I've got it! Ascensiono!

(He points his wand to the sky. An awful screech as an owl plummets and squishes into the ground. It most certainly has died. A sound

effect indicates a loss of points as all turn to look at Oliver and Wayne in horror and disappointment.)

OLIVER RIVERS: I can't lose any more points, Wayne. Everyone hates us enough already.

WAYNE HOPKINS: Look. It's Halloween! Let's just sit back, relax, and hope nothing bad happens.

(Professor Turban runs on. The music screeches and ends.)

PROFESSOR TURBAN: T...T...T...Troll! In the dungeon!

(Professor Turban runs off. A beat of silence. Then chaos.)

PUFFS: *AHHHHHHHH! *Troll?! *TROLL! *What's a troll? *We're CONFUSED!

CEDRIC: Everyone, quick! Puffs Emergency Formation #4!

(Everyone huddles together. They put one hand on their heads for protection and they hold their wands out for who knows what. Together, they march and chant.)

PUFFS: We are not a threat. Please, be our friend? We are not a threat. Please, be our friend?

(They continue to softly chant this mantra as Harry enters ahead of them. In his hands is a mop. A mop with bright red hair. This mop is Ron. He is Ron Mop.)

HARRY: Wait! ...Ron...I've just had a thought! Hermione?!

(Harry shakes the mop to show us that Ron has some feelings on this.)

HARRY: I know that, Ron. But she doesn't know about the troll. We have to go save her!

(Harry and Ron Mop exit, as the Narrator watches them go.)

NARRATOR: Ugh. Meanwhile, in the Puff common room!

Scene: Back in The Common Room

With a sudden shift we find ourselves back in that basement near the kitchens. The Puffs are huddled close, fearing for their lives, fearing what this troll may do. Their emergency formation chant has transformed into a plea. Loud footsteps echo above them.

PUFFS: We are not a threat! Please be our friend?!

SUSIE BONES: ...It's going to kill us all!

HANNAH: Someone told me it must be my long-lost twin sister. Oh, I get it, they were bullying me.

J. FINCH: J. Finch is too young to die!

CEDRIC: Everyone, everyone! Calm down. We're safe in our basement. This will be the only time our lives will ever be in danger here. Ever. Now. I'm off to bed.

(Cedric exits. He's worked his magic over the Puffs, and they have all calmed down.)

PUFFS: *Ooo bed. *Yeah, bed. *Bed sounds nice!

(The Puffs exit. Oliver tries to leave with them.)

WAYNE HOPKINS: Oliver! Wait. Megan's not here.

OLIVER RIVERS: Oh no, does she need to be saved or something?

WAYNE HOPKINS: No! What if she's out there losing points?! We have to stop her.

OLIVER RIVERS: I'm sorry, *we?*

WAYNE HOPKINS: It's up to all of us to protect those points. This is it, Oliver. The points are how we become heroes. Let's go!

(The two exit in search of wizard shenanigans.)

Scene: A Trio Is Born

We shift to some place darker. Ominous. Spookier. A forbidden classroom in a forbidden hallway. In this classroom, there is a weird mirror. Megan Jones sneaks in holding a lantern. She eventually makes her way to the mirror.

MEGAN JONES: Wow. That corridor was full of some horrifying stuff. Ohhh, that's why it's forbidden. I get it. Whoa. Weird mirror. Whoaaaah. Demon mirror.

(Megan, for a moment, looks into the weird mirror with an air of wonder. Slowly behind her, the ghost of A Fat Friar creeps on.)

A FAT FRIAR: Boo!

MEGAN JONES: Hey! I have told you not to sneak up on me like that. Hello, Fat Friar.

A FAT FRIAR: Megan. You can just say "Friar."

(Oliver and Wayne sneak on. They hide.)

A FAT FRIAR: What are you doing all alone on Halloween? Shouldn't you be with your friends?

MEGAN JONES: Friends? You're the only person who talks to me—and oh my Wizard God—I just realized how pathetic that is.

A FAT FRIAR: Ouch. My self-esteem.

MEGAN JONES: It's just like, come on, Mom, break out of wizard prison already and come rescue me from this hellhole, *please.* I wonder what she's doing...

(The Narrator enters. Everyone freezes.)

NARRATOR: I'd like to take this moment to formally introduce you to Xavia Jones.

(A menacing witch clad in black appears and poses like a mug shot in a certain prophetic newspaper. She holds a sign with her number on it. She makes increasingly crazy faces and sounds.)

NARRATOR: A Puff. A dark wizard. They say few that have crossed her path have lived to tell the tale. I mean look at her. She looks pretty crazy. Lucky for us she is locked away in an inescapable wizard prison and will probably never get out...probably.

(Xavia and the Narrator exit.)

A FAT FRIAR: Anyway! How about a game of Wiz Checkers? Maybe those two sneaky boys want to join?

OLIVER RIVERS: RUN FOR YOUR LIFE!

16

MEGAN JONES: GET OUT HERE. NOW!

(Megan waves her wand. Oliver and Wayne fall into the room. A few more spells move them center.)

MEGAN JONES: So, you followed me, Hopkins? Spying on me? Trying to learn my dark evil secrets?

OLIVER RIVERS: No, uh, we were just, uh, trying to find you.

WAYNE HOPKINS: To protect you from the troll. And to make sure you don't lose any more points.

(Megan magics their hands together.)

MEGAN JONES: Do I look like I need protecting? From the two of you? Wait. A troll? Where? I want it. *As a pet.*

A FAT FRIAR: Megan, this is why you don't have any friends.

MEGAN JONES: Shut up, fatty.

A FAT FRIAR: *Self-esteem.*

MEGAN JONES: These two are going to get what they deserve. Hm. What would my mom do in a situation like this? I think she'd torture you! Prepare to meet your doom!

(Megan raises her wand to strike. Oliver screams.)

WAYNE HOPKINS: Wait! Wait! What if instead of torturing us, we all just hung out? Like friends?

OLIVER RIVERS: *We'll what?

MEGAN JONES: *Excuse me?

A FAT FRIAR: Yeaaaaah! Go for it!

WAYNE HOPKINS: Look, we're all kind of the worst people at this school. Why not be the worst together? Megan shouldn't have to be alone just because her mom was evil. And hey, I think it's cool that you hang out with Mr. Friar.

A FAT FRIAR: Heeeey, *Mr. Friar.* I like it!

WAYNE HOPKINS: Right, Oliver?

OLIVER RIVERS: Yeah. We can all hang out. Fat Friar too.

A FAT FRIAR: Awwww. My self-esteeeem!

(A Fat Friar exits, his self-esteem hurt.)

MEGAN JONES: You promise this isn't a joke?

WAYNE HOPKINS: I promise. Us Puffs have to stick together.

MEGAN JONES: I'm not a Puff. The hat got it wrong. I'm the most not-Puffiest person you'll ever meet. Got it?

(She points her wand in Wayne's face.)

WAYNE HOPKINS: Got it.

(She points it at Oliver.)

OLIVER RIVERS: Got it.
WAYNE HOPKINS: Now how about letting us go?
MEGAN JONES: ...I guess.

(Megan hesitates for a moment. She unties them using magic. She then uses her wand in a knighting-like fashion on the following:)

MEGAN JONES: I dub thee friends. ...Is that how this works? I don't really have...*friends.*
OLIVER RIVERS: Sure.
WAYNE HOPKINS: Great. Glad we've settled that, we should probably get out of here? If we're caught, we will lose so many points.

(Professor Sproutty enters and catches them.)

PROFESSOR SPROUTTY: Students lurking while a troll is about?! *The plants will be so disappointed.*
MEGAN JONES: Wait! I was hunting the troll. So, I could...shove my wand up its nose and...I don't know...*murder it.* But these two friends taught me the error of my ways.
PROFESSOR SPROUTTY: Hmm...fifty points...*to* the Puffs. Each!

(A sound effect indicates points are earned.)

PROFESSOR SPROUTTY: The plants love life lessons. Goodnight!

(Professor Sproutty exits.)

OLIVER RIVERS: *YEAH!
MEGAN JONES: *Hey!
WAYNE HOPKINS: *WE DID SOMETHING! Guys. I think this is the start of something really great.

(Wayne becomes aware of the mirror behind them.)

WAYNE HOPKINS: Whoa! *Weird mirror!*

(The Narrator enters.)

NARRATOR: Yes, a weird mirror with the power to show the greatest desire of the onlooker's heart. One must wonder what these three would see whilst looking in it? Hmmmm...

(Elements of the following "visions" play out in front of the trio in their "reflections.")

WAYNE HOPKINS: Wow. I'm being handed a medal. I saved all the wizards. I'm a hero. I'm *the* hero. I've officially made the Puffs the best, coolest, most important house forever! *(He gasps.)* And I have a lightsaber!

(Wayne's reflection holds up a green lightsaber. Excited, he steps aside. Oliver moves in front of the mirror.)

OLIVER RIVERS: I finally do it. A brand-new theorem that makes differential calculus look like trigonometry for dumb-dumbs. Awesome.

(Oliver's reflection is handed a certificate. It says MATH on it. He steps aside. Megan looks into the mirror. But she quickly backs away.)

MEGAN JONES: I, uh. I don't see anything.
OLIVER RIVERS: That's weird. Are you sure?
WAYNE HOPKINS: I don't want to cut this short, but we should probably get out of here.
OLIVER RIVERS: Yeah. What do you think this mirror is?
WAYNE HOPKINS: Maybe it shows the future? THAT MUST BE OUR FUTURE! We're going to be so cool!

(Wayne and Oliver exit as Megan hangs back. She slowly walks back and stands in front of the mirror. She smiles.)

NARRATOR: What exactly did Ms. Jones see in her reflection? Well...

(In the mirror, a loving version of Xavia stands beside Megan. She messes with her daughter's hair and hugs her.)

MEGAN JONES: It's my mom. She wants to go somewhere far away, just us. The future, huh? All right.

(Megan turns to leave but feels something in her back pocket. She pulls out a glowing red stone.)

MEGAN JONES: Whoa, how did this rock get in here?

(She throws this likely unimportant rock away. The Narrator retrieves it.)

NARRATOR: Oh. Oh my. I, uh, sadly am obligated to inform you that this was not the only lifelong friendship forged on October 31st, 1991.

(Harry bursts in with Ron Mop and Hermeoone, here just played by a wig.)

HARRY: Well, you two. It looks like we're going to be real good mates. *Forever*!
NARRATOR: WE GET IT. Jesus Merlin Christ. Some people.

(Harry smiles and slowly exits, followed by a flustered Narrator.)

Scene: Wayne & Cedric

Wayne enters with his wand out, attempting to do magic. It is not going so well.

WAYNE HOPKINS: Lumos. Lumos. Lumos.

(Cedric has entered and spots Wayne fumbling.)

CEDRIC: It's in the way you move your wrist. Like a little circle. *Lumos.*

(Cedric's wand lights up with ease.)

CEDRIC: ...*Wayne*, right?

WAYNE HOPKINS: Yes. Yeah. Yes. Yeah. Yes. Yes. Yes. Wayne. Um, hi
    Cedric.
CEDRIC: Listen, man. Winning all of those points? Pretty cool. You really
    started something. Everyone's earning points now!

(Various Puffs rush on.)

ERNIE MAC: Repairo!

(Ernie repairs something. He earns points!)

HANNAH: Alohamoro!

*(Hannah opens a door with magic. She earns points. A feather
appears.)*

J. FINCH: ***Olive Gardium Leviosa.
SALLY PERKS: ***No. It's Olive Gardium Leviosahh.

*(The feather floats. Points are earned. Leanne enters staring at her
hands.)*

LEANNE: We're wizards!

(Cedric low fives Leanne. She runs off, happy!)

CEDRIC: We're moving up. I think we're finally going to do it this year.
    THIRD PLACE!

(Cedric turns to go.)

WAYNE HOPKINS: Hey Cedric. ...Third place!

(Cedric gives a thumbs up to Wayne and exits. Wayne jumps for joy.)

WAYNE HOPKINS: Ahhhhhhhhh! Cedric thinks I'm cool. *I feel like I could
    do anything right now.* LUMOS!

(The spell does not work.)

WAYNE HOPKINS: ...I guess I'll go watch the Sports game.

Scene: Sports!

Many people enter and throw balls and hit other balls, and it is all basically chaos until Harry simply flies by and procures a small yellow ball at which point everyone exits. A voiceover lays over the top.

VOICEOVER: Sports! For those of you joining us these players are trying to throw the ball through the hoops to score points but don't get hit by those other balls AND OHP HE CAUGHT THE BALL. Game over, the Puffs lose in the shortest game ever. How sad. Sports!

Scene: The End of The Year

The First Headmaster addresses the students in the Great Hall. All the Puffs stand, giggly with anticipation.

FIRST HEADMASTER: Students! Gather round. Yes, yes. Another year! What a year it has been. Now, the House Cup must be awarded. In fourth place, the Braves with 312 points. In third place, the Puffs with—
CEDRIC: CAN I HEAR A THIRD PLACE?!
PUFFS: THIRD PLACE!

(A "We Are The Champions"-esque song plays, all about winning third place. The Puffs hug. They cry. They celebrate. The music cuts out.)

FIRST HEADMASTER: Yes, yes, well done, Snakes. Well. Done. Snakes. However, recent events must be taken into account. Now you may find yourself asking...can he give out more points now? Yes. Yes, he can.
NARRATOR: And so...The Headmaster ended up dishing out a couple of extra points for some questionable accomplishments.
OLIVER RIVERS: A chess game?
MEGAN JONES: Logic?
WAYNE HOPKINS: Pure nerve?
PUFFS: Standing up to friends?!
FIRST HEADMASTER: So, we need a change of decoration.

(The First Headmaster changes his hat from green to red.)

FIRST HEADMASTER: Haha! Oh, me.

(The First Headmaster exits, pleased with himself. The Puffs stand disappointed.)

PUFFS: Awww.
LEANNE: Hey. Don't be sad. This year we learned skills, built friendships, and nobody died except that teacher! What a year! You can't put a number on *life!* Unless you can, in which case, it's four. Fourth place for us!

(Leanne freezes midair, or at least tries to.)

PUFFS: Awwwwwwwww.
CEDRIC: But hey...we're wizards.
PUFFS: Yeaaaah!

(The Puffs exit, satisfied for now. The Narrator pulls out a book with a 2 on it.)

Scene: Year Two

NARRATOR: And that was the class of '98's first year of magic school. Now. YEAR TWO! Ah, the second year. You're older. You're wiser. You're ready for a safe, fun year. NOPE! Welcome to YEAR TWO: THE PUFFS AND THE ANCIENT GIANT SNAKE THAT BEGAN ATTACKING STUDENTS THE SAME YEAR IT WAS DISCOVERED A CERTAIN OTHER STUDENT COULD TALK TO SNAKES.

(A giant snake slithers on for a moment. The Narrator covers their eyes.)

NARRATOR: Not yet!

(The snake slithers away. Oliver enters with teachers.)

NARRATOR: First: schoolwork!

(School bell. We're in Potions class.)

A CERTAIN POTIONS TEACHER: What is this concoction you have made, *MR. RIVERS?*
OLIVER RIVERS: A potion?
A CERTAIN POTIONS TEACHER: Remedial Potions will be in order this year.

(School bell. Now we're in Professor McG's class.)

PROFESSOR McG: OLIVER! You were to transfigure this beetle into a button. What is so difficult about that?
OLIVER RIVERS: Everything?
PROFESSOR McG: Remedial Transfiguration, Oliver.

(School bell. We're in Ghost History Teach's class. He is a ghost.)

GHOST HISTORY TEACH: History of magic. Magic history. Wizards. History. Remedial History of Magic, MR. RIVERS!

(Ghost History Teach exits.)

OLIVER RIVERS: But...I'm a...I'm a smart person.

(Oliver cries to a fellow student.)

OLIVER RIVERS: I'm a smart person!

(Colin enters with a camera. Click. He takes a picture of Oliver crying.)

OLIVER RIVERS: Hey, cut it out.

(Click. Colin takes another picture.)

OLIVER RIVERS: Seriously, please leave me alone.

(Click.)

OLIVER RIVERS: GET AWAY FROM HERE NOW!

(Colin turns to leave. He turns back. Click. He exits.)

OLIVER RIVERS: I hope something really bad happens to that kid.

(The Narrator enters.)

NARRATOR: Yikes. Halloween arrived, and brought with it a nasty surprise.

(Megan enters with Wayne. Megan now wears glasses and is holding a large stack of books. The trio crosses together.)

MEGAN JONES: A Secret Chamber has been opened. There's a monster. There's a message written in blood. It's the coolest thing ever. Also, I'm into books now.

(They exit.)

NARRATOR: Naturally, less people were as excited about this.

(Professor Locky enters. He's got a nice smile.)

PROFESSOR LOCKY: I am not excited about this! It is my duty to make sure you are all educated. So! Who wants to come to DUELING CLUB?!

(All rush on around Professor Locky.)

Scene: Dueling Club & Harry Wants to Kill Everyone

PROFESSOR LOCKY: Now. None of us want to end up like that poor boy who was attacked. The one with the camera.
OLIVER RIVERS: *No. We certainly didn't want anything bad to happen to him.*
PROFESSOR LOCKY: Let's get some volunteers up here. Um, Mr. Potter.

(Professor Locky magically immediately becomes A Certain Potions Teacher.)

A CERTAIN POTIONS TEACHER: And Mr. Malfoy.

(Harry and Blondo step forward.)

BLONDO MALFOY: SNAKE SPELL!

(A snake shoots out of Blondo's wand and lands in J. Finch's hands.)

J. FINCH: Ahh! J. Finch sees a snake. J. Finch is going to die!

(Harry grabs the snake. He speaks to it. The Narrator enters.)

HARRY: Snake, no! Snake what are you doing? Don't bite Justin. Leave us
    alone.
NARRATOR: Unfortunately, this is not what the rest of the school heard.
    This is:

(Harry waves the snake at everyone.)

HARRY: SSSSaaah aGrrraaa Grraaaaassaaaaahhh!!!
J. FINCH: Harry tried to kill me!
WAYNE HOPKINS: He's going to kill everyone!

(The Puffs panic and run around.)

PUFFS: AHHHHHHHHH! AHHHH! WE ARE NOT A THREAT!

Scene: More Terror in the Common Room

This panic transitions to a fear huddle in the Puff common room.

PUFFS: *Please be our friend.*
WAYNE HOPKINS: No question about it. Potter is the Heir of Snakes.
    Someone has to stop him.
SUSIE BONES: He's going to kill us all.
J. FINCH: No. It's just ol' J. Finch he's after. And I never got...I never got
    to...I never got to eat all the flavored beans.
ERNIE MAC: Justin, we'll keep you safe. Just promise me you won't leave
    this common room. Promise us all you won't leave.
J. FINCH: I promise...Welp! I'm going to leave now, bye!
PUFFS: Bye!

(J. Finch leaves. Preferably via skipping.)

SALLY PERKS: ...Let's all go to bed?

PUFFS: *Ooo! *Bed. *Bed sounds nice. *Etc.

(All exit.)

Scene: The Heir of Snakes

J. Finch enters (maybe still skipping). He sings.

J. FINCH: J. Finch, finchin' around. Finchin' the halls. Finchin' himself!

(Mr. Nick, a ghost, enters.)

J. FINCH: Oh, hi, Mr. Nick!
MR. NICK: Hello Justin!

(The snake slithers out. J. Finch and Nick see the snake and find themselves petrified. Harry enters.)

HARRY: Uh oh! Better get out of here before someone sees me!

(Other students enter. They point at Harry, scream, and run away.)

HARRY: Nobody understands Harry!

(Harry exits. Cedric enters and sees the petrified J. Finch and Mr. Nick. Mr. Nick, frozen in horror, floats off stage as Cedric lifts up the stone-still J. Finch.)

CEDRIC: We'll get you finching around again in no time.

(Cedric carries J. Finch off as Wayne and Oliver enter, checking every corner. Megan bursts in.)

WAYNE HOPKINS: Shhhhhh! It got J. Finch. We have to be careful. Who knows what could be lurking around every corner.
MEGAN JONES: Well if all of the books I've been reading mean anything, there is definitely a monster, and it's out to kill everyone. It's super cool. I mean...meri-tori-ous. I'm into books now.
OLIVER RIVERS: This is a lot for twelve-year-olds to handle.

WAYNE HOPKINS: The adults aren't helping...so, obviously it must fall to *me* to find this monster, defeat Potter, and go down in history as the hero of the school.

OLIVER RIVERS: I don't know if you're qualified for any of that.

WAYNE HOPKINS: I'll get an award. Megan, take Oliver to safety. It's definitely coming for him next.

OLIVER RIVERS: ...What?!

MEGAN JONES: It's after Mug Borns. You're a Mug Born. Which means you're next. OH MY WIZARD GOD WHAT IS THAT?!

OLIVER RIVERS: AHHHHHH!

MEGAN JONES: Ha. Just kidding. *Wow. It's gonna be a fun year.*

OLIVER RIVERS: Wayne, if I get petrified, make sure I'm in a dignified position.

(Oliver and Megan exit. Wayne scans the room.)

WAYNE HOPKINS: Okay. This must be it. The thing I'm supposed to do to make that Magic-Future-Mirror reflection of my awesome future self my actual future. I just gotta kill a monster. *I can find it inside myself.* My inner...Robocop. My spiritual John McClane. Yeah. "Hey, Monster! Puff on this..." Pew, pew, pew.

(Ginny, a fellow student and romantic interest, enters. She too scans the room for some unknown terror, a diary clutched in her hands. Distracted, she bumps into Wayne. The diary falls to the ground. Upon eye contact, Wayne is immediately in love.)

GINNY: Oh. I'm...I'm sorry. My fault.

WAYNE HOPKINS: No! I was just... Hi. I'm Wayne.

GINNY: Ginny. My name is Ginny. It's very nice meeting you, Wayne.

(Ginny starts to exit.)

WAYNE HOPKINS: Hey, don't forget your diary.

(Ginny freaks out.)

GINNY: NOOOO! WHAT WILL IT MAKE ME DO NEXT?!

WAYNE HOPKINS: Hey, if it's so bad why don't you just put it somewhere no one will ever find it? Like a toilet or something?

GINNY: A toilet? ...*Maybe.* Thanks, Wayne.

(Ginny exits.)

WAYNE HOPKINS: Wow. I am in love. As soon as I become the hero of the school, that girl will want to marry me. This is really my year!

Scene: A Great Hall Again/End of Year Again

We find ourselves back in the Great Hall. The First Headmaster enters, A Certain Potions Teacher behind him.

FIRST HEADMASTER: Students! Gather round. Yes. Yes.

(All enter and arrange themselves to listen to The First Headmaster. J. Finch, still petrified, is carried on by Cedric.)

FIRST HEADMASTER: I just want to reaffirm to you all: even in the face of great danger, the doors of this school will always remain open.

(A Certain Potions Teacher whispers in The First Headmaster's ear.)

FIRST HEADMASTER: Never mind. A redhead's been kidnapped. School's cancelled forever. Go home.
MEGAN JONES: Yes! Forget books! Suck it everyone.

(A Certain Potions Teacher again whispers in The First Headmaster's ear.)

FIRST HEADMASTER: Never mind. The monster is dead. Let's hear a big round of applause for the boy who fought it alone...MR. POTTER!

(Harry enters with Ron Mop as all applaud.)

HARRY: Not completely alone. Ron helped. I'm the hero of the school!

(All applaud as Harry bows.)

FIRST HEADMASTER: Yes. Yes. Now, you all know I don't pick favorites. But, Harry—he's my favorite. Now, please, I would like to take a moment of silence for my pet bird who tragically died.

(A phoenix cries.)

FIRST HEADMASTER: Never mind. He's alive again. Exams are cancelled. See you next year!

(All celebrate and exit, save poor J. Finch who is still petrified. The Narrator enters.)

NARRATOR: Year Two. The one with snakes.

(The Narrator sees J. Finch. They snap their fingers and J. Finch skips off like nothing ever happened.)

J. FINCH: J. Finch, finching around!
NARRATOR: Ta da!

Scene: Letters

NARRATOR: The Summer of '93! And our trio was determined to keep in touch the old-fashioned way: by writing two copies of the same letter and then sending them by owl across the world.

(The trio each stand isolated in three separate spots. Each is at their various homes and each holds a quill. They write.)

WAYNE HOPKINS: Dear Megan & Oliver. This new movie just came out. It's called *Free Willy*. It's about a young boy's adventure to free a whale. *It was amazing.* I can't stop thinking about how adventures come in all shapes and sizes. I know mine is coming. I just have to find my own whale. I have to free my own Willy. —Wayne. P.S. HOW DOES THIS OWL KNOW WHERE TO GO?!

(We shift to Oliver.)

OLIVER RIVERS: Wayne! Yeah...sure. Free your Willy. See you soon! —Oliver.

(We shift back to Wayne, now with Uncle Dave.)

UNCLE DAVE: Uncle Dave here. There is an owl in my livin' room! HaHA! Birds!

(We shift to Megan.)

MEGAN JONES: Wayne! Oliver! ...Wayne's uncle. Willys? Whatever! Big news: a mass murderer broke out of Wizard Prison. What if my mom sent him after me?! To come and rescue me from that shitty school?! I've got a feeling...this year, things are going to be really...*Sirius.* *(Hold for uproarious laughter.)* P.S. The guy's name is Sirius.

(All exit.)

NARRATOR: A murderer on the loose? Ruh roh. But not to worry. Wizard Government safety measures have been put into effect. Something that will make the children feel...safe.

(The atmosphere all around the theater becomes chilling. Wind blows. The sound of a heart beating faster and faster. Screams. Lights go out. Slowly, Soul Sucking Security Guards appear in various places. Behind the Narrator, a giant Soul Sucking Security Guard's hands appear. The heart beat quickens. The screams get louder. The giant Soul Sucking Security Guard climbs over the walls poised to attack. The audience grips their chests in search of a happy thought. Unable to find one, they crumble in their seats. The Narrator pulls out their wand.)

NARRATOR: *EXPECTING AN EXPECTATION!*

(A flash of white light. The Soul Sucking Security Guards shriek and flee. The Narrator pulls out a ***chocolate treat and distributes it to the front row of the audience.)

NARRATOR: ...Very safe. Here, you in the front. Eat this. It's magic chocolate. A *[***name of whatever chocolate]*. It'll make you feel happy again. You in the back...I'm sorry. You're sad forever. Safety is the name of the game in YEAR THREE: THE PUFFS IN PAJAMAS, BECAUSE A MASS MURDERER GOT INTO THE SCHOOL!

Scene: Year Three

The trio stands center. Megan displays a real plucky, go-get-'em, and Brave attitude. Oliver reiterates an observation that he cannot possibly believe he is the only one who has noticed.

OLIVER RIVERS: I am telling you guys, The Headmaster looks different this year.

WAYNE HOPKINS: Oliver, I'm a little more worried about the murderer coming to our school. Megan, what if he's not coming to rescue you...what if he's coming to murder someone?!

MEGAN JONES: Nope. He's definitely coming to rescue me. It'll be a super huge deal because this year I will be spending my time with the Braves, and everything notable that happens, happens to them. Like this guy!

(Clumsy Longbottom has entered. He stands there, confused about life.)

CLUMSY LONGBOTTOM: I'm Neville? I'm Brave?

MEGAN JONES: If you need me, we will be out there being both rebellious and charming. And Brave!

(The two exit as Leanne enters and circles Wayne and Oliver. She hands out invitations.)

LEANNE: Guys! Guys! *Guys.* Come to my slumber party! It's in the Great Hall! On the floor! It's going to be so much fun. But I warn you: I snore! Want to see?

(She falls asleep. She does not snore.)

WAYNE HOPKINS: ...Leanne?

LEANNE: Sorry! I was having a dream I was a unicorn, only I didn't have a horn and I was eating hay.

OLIVER RIVERS: *Sorry, I've got a lot going on.

WAYNE HOPKINS: *Ooh, can't, I think.

LEANNE: Aw. Everyone is busy.

(Leanne exits as Sally enters. She takes one of the invitations.)

SALLY PERKS: Hmm. What's this?

WAYNE & OLIVER: Hi, Sally.
SALLY PERKS: You boys are having a slumber party? Ooh!

(Sally removes her glasses. Wayne and Oliver, thirteen-year-old boys, feel something.)

WAYNE & OLIVER: *Hi, Sally.*
SALLY PERKS: Hm. I don't have a sleeping bag. Guess I'll have to share. Hahaha.
WAYNE & OLIVER: HAHAHAHAHA!

(It dawns on Sally that this new-found love of her jokes is somehow related to her current lack of glasses. She tosses them away. She cannot see without them.)

SALLY PERKS: Guess I'll be seeing you boys...around.

(She leaves, or at least tries to. Legally blind, she takes a moment to desperately search for the exit.)

OLIVER RIVERS: Oh my, my, Sally Perks certainly 'perked up' if you know what I...uh...
WAYNE & OLIVER: I have to go.

(They exit.)

NARRATOR: In their third year, students are allowed to pick electives. Enthralling subjects such as:

Scene: Electives

School bell. Wayne enters. Throughout the following classes, Hermeoone is in each class behind whichever member of the trio is speaking. She is played by a different actor each time.

WAYNE HOPKINS: Divination! The art of seeing the future.
PROFESSOR LANNY: Oooo. The future! Ooo! The inner eye. Tea leaves. And—

(Everything shifts to be much more ominous.)

PROFESSOR LANNY: —Death. DEATH is coming. To you all! DEAAAATH!

(Everything abruptly shifts back to normal.)

PROFESSOR LANNY: *Cough* What? Class dismissed.

(School Bell. Professor Lanny becomes the Runes Teach as Megan and Hermeoone #2 enter.)

MEGAN JONES: Ancient Runes. It's about rocks.
RUNES TEACH: NOW! How old do you think this rune is? Guess what. It's ANCIENT. It's an ANCIENT RUNE.
MEGAN JONES: Is this useful in any way?
RUNES TEACH: Nope! Class dismissed forever.

(School bell. Runes Teach becomes Ms. Babble as Oliver enters with Hermeoone #3.)

OLIVER RIVERS: Arithmancy. Another class I'm sure I'll fail.
MS. BABBLE: Welcome, class, to Mug Studies.
OLIVER RIVERS: Ohp, sorry. Wrong room.
MS. BABBLE: Now can anyone tell me what this is?

(Ms. Babble holds up a picture of a toaster. Oliver slowly raises his hand.)

OLIVER RIVERS: ...That is a toaster.
MS. BABBLE: Oooh, a smarty smart. A regular Einstein—we'll cover him later. Now, can anyone tell me what algebra is?

(Oliver turns with the world's biggest grin on his face.)

OLIVER RIVERS: I'd like to stay in this class please!

(Wayne and Megan enter next to Oliver.)

WAYNE HOPKINS: Wait a second! How is Granger in all three of our classes at the same time?

(A beat of silence. They then realize...)

ALL THREE: Magic.

(They exit. The three Hermeoones enter and nearly bump into each other.)

HERMEEONES: Oh, honestly.

(They exit as the Narrator enters.)

NARRATOR: And so, the school was off to an eventful, yet safe, start. But all that would change on, you guessed it: Halloween.

(The Narrator exits as the following voiceover starts. It emulates a school overhead announcement from the "new," harsher Headmaster. Megan perks up at the news.)

SECOND HEADMASTER (V.O.): Attention, students...The Headmaster here. The murderer is in the school...he attacked a portrait then left. Report to the Great Hall! I SAID NOW!

(Megan sulks off to the side as the other Puffs enter, yawning, awoken from sleep.)

Scene: A Great Hall Slumber Party

The students enter and chant, sort of bored at this point:

PUFFS: We are not a threat. Please be our friend.

(Leanne enters, excited.)

LEANNE: Guys! Guys! THE WHOLE SCHOOL CAME TO MY SLUMBER PARTY! Why is everyone so sad and frightened?!
SUSIE BONES: That poor painting.
PUFFS: That poor painting.
HANNAH: Hey guys, someone told me that the murderer is only going after pretty girls so I don't have to worr—oh. I get it, *they were bullying me.*

(Cedric enters.)

CEDRIC: Everyone, I've been told to inform you it looks like we'll be spending the whole night here.

PUFFS: *(Sad)* Awww.

LEANNE: *Yay!

CEDRIC: But hey! How about a story to help you get to sleep?

HANNAH: Maybe a story about the Puffs?

J. FINCH: A cool one?

PUFFS: YEAH.

(The Puffs all cross their arms and show they want a cool story.)

CEDRIC: There's the story of Helga. The First Puff. That's a pretty...cool story.

(The Puffs slowly move towards Cedric and the book, because hey, cool story.)

CEDRIC: All right then. "Once upon a time..."

(The Narrator enters. We magically transition to something akin to a children's puppet show.)

NARRATOR: A professional will take it from here! From "The Tragic Yet Rewarding History of the Puffs," Chapter Two. "There once lived an excellent cook, who also happened to be a witch. Her name was Helga."

(Helga enters.)

HELGA: Have you seen my cup? It's a nice cup. Oh, badgers.

NARRATOR: "She could often be found hanging out with her special friends!"

(Rowena pops up wearing glasses. She is a puppet.)

ROWENA: Let's play a game. Who can read all the books? Whoops I won! I am so smart.

HELGA: Why don't we play a different game? That is, if you are brave enough?

(Ric Gryff bursts in, bravely. He is a puppet.)

RIC GRYFF: Did someone mention bravery in passing? Rawr.

(Sal slithers on. He is a puppet.)

SAL: SSSSSAAAAAAaaaaaaaaaasGrassttthaaaaaaaaaaaa. Hey guys.

HELGA: We have all of this great magical knowledge, why don't we start a school?

NARRATOR: "And so, they magic'd a castle into existence. But they were left with an important question to answer: what type of students would they admit?"

RIC GRYFF: Students who are brave!

ROWENA: Students *whom* are smart!

SAL: Students who are blonde. Rich. Assholes.

(They look to Helga.)

HELGA: Students who are...um. Well, oh.

(They are interrupted by an announcement from The Second Headmaster.)

SECOND HEADMASTER (V.O.): Attention, students. It's time for sleep. Go to sleep. NOW!

(The story elements disappear, and the Puffs return to their places around Cedric.)

PUFFS: Awwww. But how does it end?

CEDRIC: It's okay. We'll finish some other time. Goodnight!

(Cedric exits.)

MEGAN JONES: Or! How about I finish it for him now? Helga was so stupid and boring, she couldn't come up with anything, so they just gave her all the dumb kids. The Puffs. The end.

LEANNE: ...Worst slumber party ever.

(The Puffs all sadly go to sleep. Wayne and Oliver step over to Megan.)

WAYNE HOPKINS: Meggaaaaan? You alright?

MEGAN JONES: I never wanted to be a Puff. Every member of my family? Puffs. We're like THE Puff family. But I've always known that I was different. There's nothing even special about Puffs. Loyalty? Being really nice? A bunch of lame, awful failures doomed to be stupid walking personality-less nobodies that no one will ever care about ever? Ugh. My mom was a Puff. But she was different. She became something bigger. She made the name Jones finally mean something other than a bunch of...*Puffs*. I thought...I knew...*I* would be different too. But...after all my hard work to make myself not a Puff, what do you know? The hat puts me with the Puffs. I did everything. I mean, I even changed my accent just so I wouldn't sound like my Puff family.

WAYNE & OLIVER: Ohhhhhh.

MEGAN JONES: It's not fair.

OLIVER RIVERS: Well, I for one am happy you were not kidnapped by a mass murderer. Or "rescued."

WAYNE HOPKINS: And, I'd like to think you've met at least two Puffs who are...kind of okay?

(Wayne and Oliver do an "Eh?" gesture.)

MEGAN JONES: Ha. Maybe. I guess. Sorry to bring the mood down. Sorry to make things so...*Sirius*. She's not coming here. Ever. I feel the need to hug. Don't tell anyone.

(Megan hugs Oliver.)

WAYNE HOPKINS: I'm coming in...

(Wayne joins the hug. Leanne wakes up and runs to join the hug too.)

LEANNE: Why are we hugging? Wait. Don't tell me. I'll figure it out.

MEGAN JONES: Hey everyone, I'm sorry I was mean. You're not stupid.

LEANNE: That's okay, right? Puff hug?!

(Everyone gets very excited. They wait for Megan's approval.)

MEGAN JONES: Fine. Puff Hug.

PUFFS: YAY! PUFF HUG!!!

(The Puffs surround Megan in a Puff hug. Another announcement.)

SECOND HEADMASTER (V.O.): Attention students! You're all safe. *We think.* Don't forget! Tomorrow you have a field trip into town. HAVE FUN!

PUFFS: FIELD TRIP!

Scene: FIELD TRIP!

A rollicking 1990's partying song. The Narrator enters with several bottles of Adult Butter Beverage. Each Puff, excited, grabs one. But how exactly does one party? The music fades as all stand in awkward silence. Eventually, Hannah tries to fill the void.

HANNAH: Hey guys...that Sirius guy. I hear he can turn into a...uh...flowery shrub…it's true.
PUFFS: *(Feigning interest)* Ohhh.

(All slowly take a drink. Blackout. Lights come back up on VERY DRUNK CHILDREN.)

ERNIE MAC: I heard a rumor that our new teacher. He's a were-...
      A were-…
SALLY PERKS: Aware of what?!

(All laugh. This is the funniest thing that they have ever heard. Blackout. Lights up on Leanne balancing a bottle on her head while Cedric points his wand at it. Everyone watches, unsure of how this will go.)

CEDRIC: Hold still.
PUFFS: Ahhhhh…

(Cedric lowers his wand. Leanne keeps fidgeting. Cedric raises the wand.)

CEDRIC: Hold still.
PUFFS: Ahhhh…

(Cedric lowers his wand. A pause. He quickly raises it, and EVERYONE SCREAMS. Blackout. Lights up on everyone crying. J. Finch leans on Cedric's shoulder.)

J. FINCH: I have flashbacks to my petrified days. I never want to sleep again.
      J. Finch has slept enough for a lifetime.
SUSIE BONES: I know how you feel. Life is a nightmare.
PUFFS: Yeah.

(Leanne has somehow found her way into the audience or somewhere surprising.)

LEANNE: Guys?! I don't know how I got out here?!
PUFFS: YEAH!

(Party music returns. What a fun time.)

WAYNE HOPKINS: HEY! To the Puffs, and to getting totally butterbuzzed!
PUFFS: BUTTERBUZZED!
OLIVER RIVERS: Anyone know what place we're in for the House Cup this year?
MEGAN JONES: Do you even have to ask?
LEANNE: FOURTH PLACE!
PUFFS: FOURTH! PLACE!!!

(The Narrator enters as Puffs slip, shuffle, and push past, butter-drunk.)

NARRATOR: Year Three—oh. Oh, oh my. YOU ARE THIRTEEN!—

(All are gone.)

NARRATOR: —concluded. Now...we've been having a good time so far, right? I must warn you. *Fate:* it's never kind to a hero. But who does fate hate even more? *The side characters.*

Scene: Letters, Again

The trio stand in their various letter writing spots. Megan entertains herself with something from the Mug-world. A gift from her friends.

WAYNE HOPKINS: Dear Megan & Oliver, so um, my Uncle Dave died. It was sudden and weird. Weird because I don't think anybody really cared? No one really knew him. I barely even did. In the end he was just some dead...*unimportant* guy. I don't want that to happen to me. I want to be a part of something big, something important at least once in my life. Weird. –Wayne.
OLIVER RIVERS: Wayne, at least our fourth year will be starting soon, and you can forget about death for a while. –Oliver.

(They exit.)

NARRATOR: Yes, back to school. Where nothing dangerous ever happens.

Scene: Goblets. Fires.

The Second Headmaster enters. A bit grizzlier. A bit less soft spoken.

SECOND HEADMASTER: Attention, students! Same headmaster, here. This year we will be hosting two other wizard schools. One with French people...

(Frenchy Delacour enters. She's very French. She speaks with a French accent. France. Got it?)

FRENCHY: Bonjour, je suis très supérieure. Ooo, Baguette.

(A magical baguette appears in her hands.)

SECOND HEADMASTER: And the Drago-Strang Institute. They are all very intimidating, and they break dance.

(Viktor enters. He's very intimidating.)

VIKTOR: I cannot be defeated. If he dies, he dies.
SECOND HEADMASTER: They are here to compete alongside one of you in a very dangerous Wizard Tournament. Anyone who wishes to participate, put your name in this cup. We'll draw names on Halloween!

(A cup with fire flowing out of it appears. It is the Cup of Fire. The Narrator pulls out Book Four.)

NARRATOR: It only gets more exciting in YEAR FOUR: THE PUFFS AND THE YEAR THEY MATTERED!

(The Narrator holds the Cup of Fire as all students enter the Great Hall.)

SECOND HEADMASTER: It's Halloween! Let's find out who our competitors will be.

MEGAN JONES: Whoever it is, we're stuck focusing on them for the entire year. If this school has taught me anything, we're going to be disappointed.

PUFFS: *(Not excited.)* Yeah.

(Fire spews out of the cup. Or what we will call "fire." A piece of paper appears as well. The Second Headmaster takes it and reads it.)

SECOND HEADMASTER: Ow! Hot! Fire! ...*Mr. Diggory.*

(A beat of silence. What did he say? He couldn't have said. Did he— THE PUFFS FREAK OUT.)

PUFFS: AHHHHHHHH!

(Cedric walks off to blaring guitars and rock music.)

PUFFS: Cedric, Cedric, Cedric!

WAYNE HOPKINS: Omigosh. This is it! *The* big thing I've been waiting for! This is our turn in the limelight. This year is all about the Puffs! And no one can take it from us!

(Surprising to all, another name shoots out of the cup. And FIRE! More "fire" too. The Second Headmaster grabs it.)

SECOND HEADMASTER: Ow—hot. Fire…again. ...Mr. Potter?

(A stunned silence.)

SECOND HEADMASTER: MR. POTTER!!!!!!!!!!!!!!!!!!!!!!!!!

(Harry walks up sheepishly.)

HARRY: Uh oh. What'd I get into this time?

SECOND HEADMASTER: HARRY!!

(After that outburst of anger, The Second Headmaster takes a breath and speaks in a calm and collected tone.)

SECOND HEADMASTER: Did you put your name in that little ol' cup over there? Did you? I'm the definition of calm right now.

(Harry scampers off. The Second Headmaster follows, amused. Oh, Harry. The Puffs are a little bummed out.)

PUFFS: Aww.

WAYNE HOPKINS: Never mind that. We have a job to do. We have to make sure the right winner wins. Potter's had his turn. Cedric is our champion!

PUFFS: Cedric!!!

(The Puffs surround Wayne, pumped up, breathing heavy. They've never felt as frenzied.)

WAYNE HOPKINS: Great. Let's go make some badges?

PUFFS: Badges!

(All exit but Oliver, who calls out after them.)

OLIVER RIVERS: Wait, I'm president of Mug Studies club, and I was hoping some of you would maybe join...

(Harry enters with Ron Mop. They are in the midst of an angry and sincere fight.)

HARRY: Ron?! No, I didn't—RON! Oh? Is that what you think, Ron? Well, fine, Ron. I guess we're not friends. Not anymore.

(Harry throws Ron to the ground and exits. Oliver stands and looks at this dejected mop. He picks up Ron Mop in an attempt to cheer him up through polite conversation. Ron Mop will have none of that.)

OLIVER RIVERS: Hi. I'm sure you two are going to be all right. Whoa, okay. Calm down. Hey, there's no need to be an asshole. Yeah well you can bloody hell yourself! **You really are the worst member of your family.

*(**Feel free to say what you'd like for that final line. Oliver exits with Ron Mop.)*

Scene: Not Forgivable Curses

Puffs rush on, chanting "Cedric." They wear pro-Cedric badges. Real Mr. Moody enters. He has an eye. A big eye. Like, that eye is really all anyone should look at. Is it rude to look at the eye?

REAL MR. MOODY: All right, class, settle down. SETTLE DOWN! Today's lesson: curses that are...not forgivable. Trust me. Because I am the ordinary. NOT fake. Moody. Got it?

PUFFS: Yes, Real Mr. Moody.

REAL MR. MOODY: Now, there's a curse where you control people.

PUFFS: Ooh.

REAL MR. MOODY: There's a curse where you hurt people.

PUFFS: Ahhh.

REAL MR. MOODY: And, there's a curse that kills. We'll call it the Green Light Curse. Because when you use it there's a bright green light. AVADA KEDABRA!

PUFFS: AHHHHHH!!!

(He points his wand to the sky as a bright green light illuminates the stage.)

REAL MR. MOODY: Now who wants to see me mess with some spiders?

(Everyone follows Real Mr. Moody off.)

Scene: Days Before the First Task

Cedric enters, practicing. Leanne, Hannah, and J. Finch turn to watch. Rita Scooter, journalist and expertly named character, joins them.

LEANNE, J. FINCH, & HANNAH: Oooo!

LEANNE: Cedric! Are you ready for the First Task?!

CEDRIC: I think I was born ready. Bearspell!

(A teddy bear magically appears in Leanne's hands. Everyone is amazed. They applaud.)

J. FINCH: Cedric! Are you nervous?

CEDRIC: I'll be nervous once it's over. Erectio!

(Erectio is a spell which straightens an object or erects a structure. Therefore, something in J. Finch's hands straightens out or erects itself. Meanwhile, something within his pants does the same. He hides it with his cloak. Magic. Wow. Amazing.)

J. FINCH: Oh! *WHAT THE?*
RITA SCOOTER: But, Cedric. Will you win?
CEDRIC: Hm. Repairio!

(Hannah holds up a pair of glasses she was holding.)

HANNAH: He fixed these glasses I was holding!
LEANNE, J. FINCH, & HANNAH: Woooow.
CEDRIC: Getting to compete against three great wizards, and learn all about other wizard cultures? I think I already won.
LEANNE, J. FINCH, & HANNAH: Awwww.

(Wayne runs on with a large notebook.)

WAYNE HOPKINS: Hey, uh, Cedric. I was wondering if you had a minute?
CEDRIC: Sure. I'll see you all later.
HANNAH & J. FINCH: *Bye, Cedric! *Good luck!
LEANNE: You're a wizard, Cedric!

(They exit.)

CEDRIC: Hi, Wayne!
WAYNE HOPKINS: Uh, hi. So. I've been staying up all night, not all night, but all night, and sort of reading up on past tournaments to figure out what sort of creatures they might throw at you for the First Task.
CEDRIC: I definitely won't say no to help. Give me a few of them.

(Wayne opens his notebook. Each "creature" has an associated page that we see with a drawing and writings about it.)

WAYNE HOPKINS: Okay! So, uh, in 1792 they had to catch cockatrices. What would you do?
CEDRIC: Hm. I would...use magic! Aviafors!

(A bird appears in Wayne's hand. He screams in surprise and throws it off stage.)

WAYNE HOPKINS: You're not wrong. How about an angry Vila?

CEDRIC: Walk up to her. Gently move a strand of hair behind her ear. Take her hand. And show her just why they call me Diggory. Then use magic. Cheerio!

(Hannah, Leanne, and J. Finch have popped their heads out again during Cedric's sensual line. They pass out after "Diggory" and are relieved upon use of this spell. Happy, they exit.)

WAYNE HOPKINS: Awesome.

CEDRIC: Aviafors!

(Another bird appears in Wayne's hands. He throws it off stage.)

WAYNE HOPKINS: Oh. ...*Awe...some?* Ok, um I should also add that I don't completely know a lot about fantastical beasts, or even where one might find them. So, I threw in some crazy things that might exist. Like a Balrog!

(He flips to a page with a Balrog. Cedric does not know what this is.)

WAYNE HOPKINS: Or, ooh! Beholders. Not real? Darn. Or... ***Mr. Snuffalupagus?

(Whatever this may be, Wayne is a little embarrassed and confused as to why he added it.)

CEDRIC: Hey. Can I see that?

(Cedric flips through the book. It is upside down.)

CEDRIC: Wow. This is really in depth. What ancient language is this?

(Wayne moves it right side up.)

CEDRIC: Oh. I see. Modern English. *Right.* Do you mind if I hang on to this?

(Cedric turns to a page with another pop culture creature on it and holds it in just such a way that we can see it. Perhaps it is a Dalek. Perhaps it is anything else that will get the wonderful nerds excited.)

WAYNE HOPKINS: Please. Definitely. Thanks for letting me help you!
CEDRIC: Thank me? Thank you! Aviafors!

(One more bird appears. Over it, Wayne throws it off stage.)

CEDRIC: If I manage to win this thing, I'm telling everyone it was because of your help.
WAYNE HOPKINS: I...cool.

(Harry enters in a tizzy and runs past Wayne.)

HARRY: Excuse me. Cedric. CEDRIC!! Dragons! It's dragons. Anything else you've prepared for, forget it. Dragons!

(Harry closes the notebook for Cedric and exits in a panic.)

CEDRIC: Thanks! Hey, you all should probably stop wearing those badges. Harry, wait up! *I told them to stop wearing the badges!*

(Cedric chases after Harry.)

WAYNE HOPKINS: Dragons are on page 256! They eat dogs if that helps?

(Professor McG enters. In her hands are three sad birds, who never asked to exist.)

PROFESSOR McG: *Who is throwing all of these birds?!*
WAYNE HOPKINS: I better get a good seat.

(Wayne runs off.)

Scene: The First Task

The Narrator enters.

NARRATOR: And finally! It was time for the First Task! Listen to that CROWD!!!!

(The Puffs enter decked out in yellow. They sit amongst the audience. They distribute a few flags to any lucky folks seated nearby. Everyone buzzes. This event is huge. Mr. Bagman enters.)

MR. BAGMAN: Microphonus.

(He pulls out a microphone.)

MR. BAGMAN: Ladies and gentlemen. Welcome to the 1994 THREE WIZARD TOURNAMENT! Now. Are. You. READY?! Then let's hear it for your first champion...

(Epic entrance music.)

MR. BAGMAN: Weighing in at 12 1/4 inches, with the hair of a unicorn. Hailing from the quaint town of St. Catchpole. He's a prefect in the streets. He's a seeker in the sheets. Put your hands together for this sixth year...MR. DIGGORY!

(Cedric enters. All cheer.)

MR. BAGMAN: Cedric! You must obtain the golden egg on the field. But in order to do so, first: you'll have to get past this highly dangerous DRAGON!

(Entrance music fit for a '90's WWF wrestler. The Dragon enters. All boo. The Dragon, ever the heel, taunts the audience. A wrestling bell dings.)

MR. BAGMAN: It's time to BEGIN!

(The Puffs chant.)

PUFFS: CEDRIC CEDRIC HE'S OUR MAN IF HE CAN'T DO IT WE'LL STILL BE HAPPY WE HAD THIS CHANCE! GO CEDRIC!
CEDRIC: Igneous Canineitaro!

(Cedric points his wand at a rock held by the Narrator. It changes into a dog! The Dragon is distracted by it, because lunch.)

WAYNE HOPKINS: Hey! He just turned that rock into a dog! That was from my book! HE READ MY BOOK!! AHHHH!

CEDRIC: Yes, dragon. Go after the nice doggy. Eat the nice doggy.

MR. BAGMAN: Cedric has turned a rock into an adorable barking puppy to distract the dragon.

(Cedric runs past the Dragon. The Dragon rips the dog's head off.)

MR. BAGMAN: Oh MY GOD, the dragon has ripped the head off the dog, and there is now a dead dog on the field. The dragon has turned on Cedric. Cedric is on fire! Do not be confused by the tone of my voice, he is literally on fire! ANNNNNNND! He's got the egg!

(Cedric enters scorched and holds a golden egg above his head. The Puffs erupt in applause. They rush the stage and surround Cedric. They hoist him on their shoulders. NOTE: if doubling Mr. Bagman with Viktor, the following line can be recorded as a voiceover to facilitate a quick change.)

MR. BAGMAN: Need I remind everyone that there is still a dragon. Right there.

(The Dragon re-appears and roars. All scream, celebrate, and exit.)

PUFFS: AHH! Yay! AHH! Yay!

NARRATOR: The results of the First Task. Cedric came in a very exciting second place! Frenchy, she came in third.

(Frenchy and Viktor enter. Frenchy puts the Dragon to sleep, and Viktor is his intimidating self to it.)

FRENCHY: Dragon, s'endormir. Baguette.

NARRATOR: Viktor tied for first.

VIKTOR: I must break you.

NARRATOR: And whom did Viktor tie with?

(Harry jumps out.)

HARRY: I did it. I got the golden egg. Against all odds, I did it!

(Harry snuggles with the Dragon and exits. Oh, Harry.)

NARRATOR: And that, my friends, is the story of how four dragons were tricked into believing one of their children had been stolen from them.

(The Dragon exits, crying. Oliver, Megan, and Wayne enter.)

NARRATOR: Now that the highly dangerous First Task was done, the time had come for something truly terrifying: a school dance.

Scene: Dates for the Ball

Lightning strikes. Thunder.

OLIVER RIVERS: A school dance? No. Not going.
WAYNE HOPKINS: We have to. To support Cedric!
MEGAN JONES: But. *A school dance.*
OLIVER RIVERS: We have to find dates. Who would want to go with us?!
WAYNE HOPKINS: Well...I kind of have one person in mind...

(Ginny enters. Wayne looks back to Oliver and Megan.)

OLIVER RIVERS: Go for it!
MEGAN JONES: Yeah, come on. What's the worst that could happen?

(Wayne takes a breath, musters his courage, and approaches Ginny. Clumsy Longbottom enters.)

WAYNE HOPKINS: *Ginny...
CLUMSY LONGBOTTOM: *Ginny, will you go to the ball with me?
GINNY: Sure, Neville! Hi, Wayne.

(Ginny and Clumsy exit together.)

MEGAN JONES: Yikes. If it makes you feel better, that Longbottom kid...he's ugly. And he'll probably stay ugly forever.
WAYNE HOPKINS: While true, that doesn't help me find a date to the ball!
OLIVER RIVERS: How about this? Right now, forget her, forget nerves, and just ask the next person you see.
WAYNE HOPKINS: Okay.

(Leanne rushes on and stands directly in front of Wayne.)

LEANNE: Hiiii!

OLIVER RIVERS: Leanne, Wayne here has a question.

LEANNE: A question, what's that?

OLIVER RIVERS: It's what you literally just...Wayne?

WAYNE HOPKINS: Leanne, has anyone asked you to the ball yet?

LEANNE: Just my imaginary friend, J. Finch Fletchley. But I said no because...he's imaginary.

(J. Finch has entered. He hears this strange revelation. Could it be true? He looks at his hands, hoping to find proof he's real. How can he be sure? Defeated, he exits.)

WAYNE HOPKINS: Well, would you like to go with me?

LEANNE: Sure! I'll go get readyyyyyyy!

(She exits to get ready. Wayne calls after her.)

WAYNE HOPKINS: It's still like a week a—okay. Now *you* have to ask the first person you see.

OLIVER RIVERS: Okay.

(He immediately makes eye contact with Megan.)

MEGAN JONES: *AHH!

OLIVER RIVERS: *AHH! Megan. You definitely don't have a date right?

MEGAN JONES: Not how I would have started this.

OLIVER RIVERS: We could go. You know. Together?

(J. Finch enters again, still in crisis. He waves his hands in front of Wayne, praying he can see him. His existence is at stake.)

MEGAN JONES: Hmm. Better you than some other loser I guess. Better than...Mr. Imaginary.

(J. Finch's soul is crushed. His spirit breaks. He is not real, and never has been. He comes to terms with this rather quickly, and defeat turns to mischief.)

J. FINCH: J. Finch doesn't exist. *J. Finch can go wherever he wants.*

(J. Finch exits to wherever he wants.)

WAYNE HOPKINS: All right then. We are people with dates!
OLIVER & MEGAN: Yeah. Dates!

(Harry enters and places himself amongst the trio.)

HARRY: I'm not. I want to ask Cho. But I'm so embarrassed.
OLIVER RIVERS: Bye, Wayne! Hurry...

(Megan and Oliver exit, leaving Wayne with Harry. Harry slowly turns to Wayne. He smiles, his own inner monologue having some sort of unheard thought. Harry hugs Wayne. For a little too long. Then another page of line variations...this can change nightly. PICK ONE, HARRY! After ONE of those is said and Harry exits, Cedric enters, confused by Harry.)

HARRY:
(OPTION 1) Say. Remember Year Two? I talked to a spider. He was mean though. He tried to eat me! Then a car saved me. Wow. Fun times for all of us, right? Bye, Wayne! Cedric! I talked to a spider and now I'm talking to—

(OPTION 2) Say. Have you ever noticed how the end of the school year is so much busier than the rest of the year? Is it just me or is it like, come on, let's split up all this drama, am I right? Am I right? I mean...what's the deal...with that? Phew. Crazy. Bye, Wayne! Cedric. The end of the year is gonna be crazy.

(OPTION 3) Hey! Remember that flying car I had in Year Two? That was pretty crazy, right?! Bye, Wayne! Vroom Vroom! Honk Honk Cedric! Vroom!

(OPTION 4) Hey! Remember in Year Two when that teacher removed all my bones? My arm was like this. Remember? Now! I have new bones! I HAVE NEW BONES! THEY GREW THEM. Bye, Wayne! Cedric, look at my new bones!

(OPTION 5) Boy. I've had a rough couple of years, huh? All those evil people and monsters. And last year, I didn't have a permission slip to go into town. That was a real bummer for me and my life. But now I have a permission slip. I got it from...someone. *(Winks.)* Don't need one for any of the other crazy things that happen here, though. Oh well. Bye, Wayne! Cedric! I have a permission slip.

(OPTION 6) Want me to get my invisible cloak? It makes me invisible. Sometimes I use it to sneak around and take books and break all the rules! It fits twooooo. Wink. Bye, Wayne! Hey, Cedric, let me know if you want to see my cloak. But you can't see me in it. Ha!

(OPTION 7) I went to the big Sports Cup over the summer! It was great. I got there by touching a boot! Wow. BOOTS CAN TAKE YOU ANYWHERE. Welp. Bye, Wayne! Hi, Cedric. Nice boots.

(OPTION 8) Say...remember the First Task? That was pretty crazy. At first, I was like, "oh no," but then I was like "broom!" And then I was like "vroom vroom," but then the dragon broke off his chain and chased me all around the school and almost killed a bunch of people. Hahaha—ahhh. Remember that? Feels like ages ago. Bye, Wayne! Cedric, look out for that dragon! Just kidding.

WAYNE HOPKINS: HEY! Cedric! Congratulations on the First Task!
CEDRIC: Thanks, Wayne. Up top!

(Wayne is super happy to high five.)

WAYNE HOPKINS: So, you got a date to the ball yet?
CEDRIC: No. I'm more preoccupied with figuring out this golden egg. I've done everything. I tried opening it...
WAYNE HOPKINS: ...Is that it?
CEDRIC: Yeah. It just screams. Watch.

(He opens the egg. It just screams, "AHH! AHH! AHH!" He closes it, and the annoying scream ceases.)

WAYNE HOPKINS: Maybe it's a riddle? I used to work through riddle books in the...bathtub.
CEDRIC: A bathtub? Would that really help?

(Real Mr. Moody pops in.)

REAL MR. MOODY: Diggory. Use the bathtub. Trust me.

(Real Mr. Moody exits.)

CEDRIC: All right. Bathtub it is. Thanks, Real Mr. Moody! See you, Wayne.

WAYNE HOPKINS: Cedric! I hear Cho is interested in going to the ball with you. You should ask her.
CEDRIC: Hm. Sure, why not! Thanks, mate!

(Cedric exits.)

WAYNE HOPKINS: Ha. *Mate.* He might have asked her on his own. Eventually. I just helped...*I helped!*

Scene: A Bathroom

The Narrator enters. Throughout the following, the cast assembles and creates a bathroom. It is a dance. Like a ballet. And most importantly, it gives Cedric enough time to change.

NARRATOR: Imagine a bathroom. A fancy bathroom. The nice toilets. The decorative sinks. A bathtub. An enormous bathtub. A bathtub so big, if you had friends over they'd say, "Yeah, wow, that's a big tub. I don't know why I doubted you about the size of this tub. Why do we keep coming in here, Craig?" You know, a bathroom. Now imagine a seventeen-year-old boy.

(Cedric enters wearing a towel.)

NARRATOR: Yes. Let's watch this seventeen-year-old boy use the bathroom.

(The Narrator takes off Cedric's towel. He wears a pair of shorts or something. Probably.)

CEDRIC: Hello, bathtub!
BATHROOM (ALL ON STAGE): Hello, Cedric.
CEDRIC: All right. Tub! Egg! Tell me your secrets.

(He opens the egg. It just screams more. The screams attract the attention of a young ghost girl.)

MYRTLE: Waaaaah! Waaaaaah! Stop that dreadful...oh. Hello. Helllooo!
CEDRIC: Uh. Hi. My name's Cedric. You're Myrtle, right?
MYRTLE: Hehehe, you know who I am?

CEDRIC: Say, you wouldn't have any ideas how to make this egg tell me its secrets? I was told a bath would help.

MYRTLE: Who told you that?

CEDRIC: This guy named Wayne. You know how sometimes you just meet someone and you can tell they're going to be great? That's Wayne. Loyal to a tee. A real Puff.

MYRTLE: Oh.

CEDRIC: I mean that in a good way.

MYRTLE: Ohhhh! Well, enough about him. Let's just talk about us. Here. Alone. Myrtle lonely, Cedric. Myrtle wants to moan.

CEDRIC: I'm going to go underwater now! Bye!

(Cedric ducks down, and the stage is illuminated in blue. We're all underwater now. The bathroom sings a song.)

BATHROOM: MERMAIDS. STEAL YOUR FRIENDS. ...MERMAIDS!

(Cedric resurfaces.)

CEDRIC: I get it now. *Dragons, again!

MYRTLE: *Mermaids!

CEDRIC: ...Mermaids! Yes. Thanks, Myrtle!

MYRTLE: Anything for you, Cedric. You're so cool.

CEDRIC: Thanks. Bye, bathtub!

BATHROOM: Bye, Cedric!

(Cedric exits.)

MYRTLE: Goodbye, Cedric. Think of me every time you see a toilet. Waaaaaahhhhhhhh!

(Myrtle exits to the sound of sleigh bells as the bathroom disassembles and exits.)

NARRATOR: Wait. Do you hear that sound? It's BRITISH CHRISTMAS! Happy Christmas, everyone!

THE AUDIENCE (HOPEFULLY): HAPPY CHRISTMAS!!!

NARRATOR: Thank you, everyone. Now, after a day of eating sweets and opening presents, some containing...*ugh...personalized sweaters.*

(Harry enters holding Ron Mop who wears a personalized sweater.)

NARRATOR: He is so poor.

(Ron Mop is sad. Harry and Ron Mop exit.)

NARRATOR: Anyway! It was time for the ball! DJ!

Scene: The Yule-Tide Ball

A nice little slow song comes on. The Puffs enter in couples and start dancing. Leanne "dances" with Wayne, or something like it. Hannah stands in a corner by herself, but she's having a fine time. Oliver and Megan enter last—they stand against the wall.

OLIVER RIVERS: Look at everyone. Dancing. I've only been to one dance before. It was with my mom. It was normal. It was a mother/son dance. Everyone was there with their moms.
MEGAN JONES: You are such a loser.

(A moment of awkward silence.)

OLIVER RIVERS: *How about we? Nope.
MEGAN JONES: *Do you want to? Never mind.
OLIVER RIVERS: You, uh. You look nice.
MEGAN JONES: Well. I tried. I actually tried. This is your fault.
OLIVER RIVERS: This year. It's been nice to. It's just. This year you've been. Yourself. And you are...neat. Real neato.
MEGAN JONES: Thank you.

(She punches him in the arm.)

MEGAN JONES: Don't you dare tell anyone I accepted that compliment.
OLIVER RIVERS: I won't. Ow.

(More awkward silence.)

MEGAN JONES: Should we just. Let's...I'm not your mom, but...
OLIVER RIVERS: Sure.

(A very short slow dance song plays. Enough time for the two to have a nice little moment that ends far too soon. The lyrics could simply be, "A Very Short Slow Dance Song.")

OLIVER & MEGAN: That was a very short slow dance song.

(A much more upbeat song begins to play. Cedric enters.)

CEDRIC: Hey! Everyone! Let's show them how the Puffs party! Emergency formation #7!

(Straight out of a '90's movie, a short, choreographed Puff dance happens. At the end, in an attempt to match the rhythm of the music:)

PUFFS: PUFFS! ROLLCALL!
CEDRIC: Cedric!

(All Puffs say their name on a beat. Or they try to. It goes off the rails very quickly. Leanne just sort of repeats hers over and over trying to find the right spot. Megan stays quiet until the end...)

MEGAN JONES: ...Megan.
CEDRIC: *Close.* All right, I'm off to bed!
PUFFS: OOH! BED!

(The Puffs exit.)

Scene: The Second Task & the Subtleties of Lake Watching

Airhorn! The Puffs enter. They are in the stands, enthusiastic for the spectacle of the Second Task. We hear Mr. Bagman's voice overhead.

MR. BAGMAN (V.O.): Ladies and Gentlemen, squibs and squabs! Get ready for the eventful, entertaining, visually exciting SECOND TASK! Your champions have one hour to find something that has been lost. In that lake. Spoiler alert: it's their friends. On your mark. Get set. GO!

(A splash! Everyone watches with huge smiles. What fun! How amazing. A long beat of silence. The excitement and smiles slowly fade with the realization that they are all just staring at a lake and that is what they will be doing for the next hour. A fair amount of time passes before Wayne speaks.)

WAYNE HOPKINS: We are just staring at a lake...just looooking at a lake.

(Another long stretch of silence as they wonder what is happening beneath that lake. Sally points at something!)

SALLY PERKS: Oh! ...No. ...I thought I saw something. ....I did not.

(More silence.)

LEANNE: I swam in a lake once. But then I got thirsty and almost drowned. Ahh! A lake!

(Leanne runs off in fear. Everyone continues to just watch that lake. Eventually, the Narrator enters.)

NARRATOR: One hour later: the results! Frenchy failed horribly!

(Frenchy enters.)

FRENCHY: Pardon moi.
NARRATOR: Followed by Vicky, who turned into a shark. Very nice.

(Viktor enters, a shark head on his head.)

VIKTOR: I win for me! FOR ME!

(Harry enters.)

NARRATOR: And while he should be given third place, the judges decided to award Harry second, because he was nice to French people.
HARRY: **De nada!
NARRATOR: This tied him in first overall with none other than...
PUFFS: CEDRIC! CEDRIC, CEDRIC, CEDRIC!
NARRATOR: The Third Task was months away, and everyone collectively remembered: oh yeah, this is a school. Maybe we should study?
PUFFS: *Yep. *We should study. *Oh, yeah! *We're at school!

(All exit but Wayne.)

Scene: Wayne & Cedric

The Narrator holds a book out. Wayne points his wand at it and attempts to summon it. He fails.

WAYNE HOPKINS: Asio book. Asio book. BOOK, come here. Pleaseio? GAH! I HATE YOU, BOOK. YOU ARE THE WORST, BOOK. YOU SUCK, BOOK.

(Cedric has entered and watched Wayne yell at this book.)

CEDRIC: Are we yelling at books, Wayne? HEY, BOOK! YOU'RE DUMB. Ha! That is fun.
WAYNE HOPKINS: Ha. No, just trying to summon it.
CEDRIC: Ah, year four, pretty difficult tests. Asio book.
NARRATOR: Oh, yeah.

(The Narrator throws the book into Cedric's hands. Cedric knows this book.)

CEDRIC: Hey. "The Tragic Yet Rewarding History of the Puffs."
WAYNE HOPKINS: You make it look so easy.
CEDRIC: Try again.

(Cedric holds the book out. Wayne points his wand.)

WAYNE HOPKINS: Asio book!

(Nothing. A failure.)

CEDRIC: You know what the best part of being a Puff is, besides being so close to the kitchens? You fail. A lot. You fail and fail. You fail over here. You fail over there. And then you fail a lot more. But failure, Wayne, is just another form of practice. As long as you never stop trying. So...try again.

(Wayne concentrates. Cedric holds the book.)

WAYNE HOPKINS: Asio book!

(Nothing. But, after a moment, Cedric tosses the book to Wayne with a smile.)

CEDRIC: Eventually...you get better. You should hang on to that book. It can help whenever you're feeling, well, like a failure. It certainly helped me.

WAYNE HOPKINS: Ha. I'll need it. I suck at magic.

CEDRIC: ...How about this? To thank you for all your support, once the Third Task is done, I'll teach you everything I know.

WAYNE HOPKINS: Really?

CEDRIC: I'd be happy to.

WAYNE HOPKINS: Wow. We'll be like a wizard Batman and Robin.

CEDRIC: Bat...Man?

WAYNE HOPKINS: He's a...it's from a thing.

CEDRIC: *Which half is the bat?*

WAYNE HOPKINS: Don't worry about it.

CEDRIC: Hey, I better get going. I'll see you around.

(Cedric starts to exit.)

WAYNE HOPKINS: Cedric! Good luck on the Third Task.

(Cedric stops and smiles. He gives Wayne another thumbs up.)

CEDRIC: I'll be fine.

(He exits. Wayne looks to his book.)

WAYNE HOPKINS: Yes! Yes! Take that, book.

Scene: The Third Task

The Narrator enters. Behind them, the Puffs fill the stands. They are decked out in even more yellow.

NARRATOR: It was a warm June evening. The Third Task was well underway, and the crowd sat with bated breath. It had come down to two. That night, one would become a champion, and *the other*...the other would lose.

MEGAN JONES: Come on! It's been hours. How hard is it to get through a maze?

LEANNE: Very hard!

WAYNE HOPKINS: Shhhhh!!!

J. FINCH: Anyone want to hear a riddle? What has eight legs? It's a spider!

WAYNE HOPKINS: EVERYONE, quiet! I want to be able to remember the exact moment Cedric comes out of that maze.

(Suddenly, sounds and lights signify something exciting is happening. A portal opens with a boom. We do not see it, but the Puffs can.)

SALLY PERKS: LOOK IT'S CEDRIC!
PUFFS: AHHHHHH!! FIRST PLACE! FIRST PLACE!
LEANNE: Wait, wait. Why's he taking a nap?
HANNAH: Wake up, Cedric! You're a winner!
PUFFS: First plaaaceeee!
WAYNE HOPKINS: ...He's dead.

(All, shocked, slowly exit. Wayne stands looking ahead. The Second Headmaster enters.)

SECOND HEADMASTER: Remember. Should a time ever come where you must choose between something that is easy or something that is right... remember a kind, sweet, *loyal* boy...and what happened to him, because he crossed the path of an evil man. Remember Cedric.

(The Second Headmaster exits. Wayne runs off. The Narrator stands somberly.)

NARRATOR: And so, a very eventful fourth year came to an eventful conclusion.

(The Narrator pulls out a box of Official Puffs Brand Souvenir Tissues.)

NARRATOR: Here. You in the front, take these. *Puffs Brand Souvenir Tissues.* Wipe away your tears. You in the back? Still sad forever. Not to worry, everyone will rediscover happiness and joy in YEAR FIVE—*OH DEAR GOD!*

(The Narrator is handed Book Five. It is a very large book. They thumb through it, daunted by its size.)

NARRATOR: THE PUFFS AND THE YEAR WE WILL GET THROUGH QUICKLY.

Scene: Welcome Back

Back in the Puff common room, the Puffs all gather, still a little bit shaken.

SALLY PERKS: Everyone. We're all still alive.

HANNAH: Now. Me and Ernie here are prefects this year. Our number one rule is: "no being too sad."

ERNIE MAC: Yeah.

(They unfurl a small "no being too sad" banner.)

HANNAH: How was everyone's summer?

SUSIE BONES: My aunt and I stared at the door *waiting*. Waiting for the Dark Lord to arrive. To kill my aunt. *To kill me.* Death waits. *IT STALKS ME!*

(She cries. A sad moment. Leanne cries too.)

LEANNE: *I went to a water park.*

J. FINCH: I'm just happy to be here with all of you. My friends. Feelings:

PUFFS: J. FINCH APPROVED!

(The Puffs all hug in one big Puff hug. Wayne enters, Adult Butter Beverage in hand. It is not his first one today. He is quite disheveled, quite butterbuzzed, and quite angsty.)

WAYNE HOPKINS: HEY! STOP HUGGING. "Welcome back, everybody."

PUFFS: Hiiii!

WAYNE HOPKINS: Hi—shut up! Just thought I'd offer some words of wisdom to all the new Puffs joining us. GUESS WHAT? WE SUCK. We're the Puffs. We're just here to die. There's no Chosen Puff hiding among us. And if there was. THEY'D PROBABLY JUST DIE. So...enjoy your *short*, meaningless lives.

(Wayne storms off with angst. After a moment of everyone standing confused, unsure what to do with this angst, Wayne re-enters.)

WAYNE HOPKINS: Oh! Oh. Also, apparently we don't have to wear uniforms anymore. You can just wear regular clothes. So. Enjoy it while you can.

(He storms off. More angst. The Puffs remove their cloaks, astonished that they can, and exit. Oliver and Megan hang back.)

OLIVER RIVERS: Soooo...he just probably needs some time.
MEGAN JONES: Yeah. I mean how long can one person be an angsty asshole?

Scene: Hopkins, Potter, & Emotions

Wayne storms on through one door, Harry the other. They are both angry. They are both filled with angst. They slam doors.

WAYNE HOPKINS: *Nobody understands.
HARRY: *Nobody understands.

(They look at each other.)

WAYNE HOPKINS: Oh. Hey.
HARRY: Oh. Sorry. I'm in a bad mood. My friends don't like it when I'm in a bad mood.
WAYNE HOPKINS: So? Fuck 'em.
HARRY: ...Fuck...them?
WAYNE HOPKINS: Yeah...if you want to be a dick all year, just be one.
HARRY: Oh! All right! YEAH. Thanks, Wayne.

(Harry offers a handshake. Wayne shakes his head. Harry understands. Harry musters his own emotions and throws a book down on the ground. He storms off. With angst. The Second Headmaster enters and sees Wayne.)

SECOND HEADMASTER: Excuse me. Oh. Um. Student. Have you seen Harry? I wanted to explain some facts about his past, and why I've been avoiding him.
WAYNE HOPKINS: Haven't seen him.
SECOND HEADMASTER: Hm. I guess it can wait until the end of the year.

(He exits. Wayne looks at the book Harry threw down. He tries to summon it.)

WAYNE HOPKINS: Asio book.

(He fails and exits. With angst.)

Scene: The Rest of Year Five

The Narrator enters.

NARRATOR: Year Five in one word: emotions. Year Five in two words: secret meetings! Even some of our Puffs were invited to join in.

(J. Finch, Hannah, Ernie, and Susie jump on, wands out.)

J. FINCH: Man, these A.A. meetings are great. Albus's Army! The A.A.!
SUSIE BONES: We must learn to protect ourselves.
HANNAH: I was just so happy to be included. I am in the group, right?
ERNIE MAC: Harry's looking over this way. Let's practice our stunning spells.

(The four get in a square formation and face off against each other. Everyone can say what they want here, really.)

J. FINCH: *Great. I'm doing the stunning. I understand.
ERNIE MAC: *I'll do the stunning. Me. Me first.
HANNAH: *I'll go first. I'm going to be good at stunning, I just know it.
SUSIE BONES: *I'll go first. I need the practice more, so I'll go first.
ERNIE MAC: Okay. 3. 2. 1.
ALL FOUR: Stupidfy!

(All four of their heads snap back and all fall to the ground, stunned. A long, still moment of just them on the ground. Eventually, all slowly sit up.)

SUSIE BONES: What happened?
J. FINCH: I think we stunned each other?
HANNAH: You mean, we did the spell? Right?!
ALL FOUR: YEAH!

(They try to four-person high five. They miss. They exit. The Narrator flips the large book from somewhere near the middle to the last pages.)

NARRATOR: And suddenly...it was May! After some standardized testing, it was time to go home.

(Megan and Oliver enter from opposite sides as the Narrator exits.)

OLIVER RIVERS: Hey! *How'd you do? Maybe okay!

MEGAN JONES: *How'd you do? Maybe okay! Yeah, I think we actually made progress this year.

OLIVER RIVERS: Yeah—we should uh, study together all the time.

MEGAN JONES: Okay, yeah, no. But you know what? I think we got through an entire year without some sort of horrible event or tragedy. It's like I almost feel...

OLIVER RIVERS: *Safe.

MEGAN JONES: *Safe.

(Megan and Oliver kiss. A sweet moment. Something that sounds like "Kiss From A Rose" might play. Wayne storms on. He sees them. Eventually, he interrupts.)

WAYNE HOPKINS: Hey!

MEGAN JONES: *AH!

OLIVER RIVERS: *Just a normal day, doing normal things.

(Megan and Oliver avoid him and nonchalantly pretend to do something else.)

WAYNE HOPKINS: Look. I'm sorry I was an angsty asshole this entire year. Can we be friends again?

(Megan walks over to him. She looks him in the eyes. She opens up her arms. They hug.)

OLIVER RIVERS: I'm coming in.

(Oliver joins the hug.)

OLIVER RIVERS: Aw. Everything is back to normal!

(Puffs pop out from various places.)

SALLY PERKS: OH NO! He-Whose-Name-We-Can't-Say is definitely back.

J. FINCH: Harry fought him. Again!

PUFFS: Nobody is safe!

(The Puffs exit.)

OLIVER RIVERS: Yep. Back to normal.

(The trio exits. The Narrator enters.)

NARRATOR: Amidst a state of national terror, Year Five was done.

(They throw the book offstage. A stage crew member is injured.)

LITERAL STAGE CREW MEMBER: Agh!

(A shift in tone to something darker. Sinister. Death Buddies begin entering, cloaked in black masks and hoods.)

NARRATOR: The world was changing. Nobody was safe. Wandmakers. Bridges. No one! *FOR THE DARK LORD HAD RETURNED!*

Scene: The Dark Lord

Mister Voldy surges on, dramatically. He stands to let us bask in his evil glory. He touches his head with his weird fingers. Death Buddies chant to their master.

DEATH BUDDIES: The Dark Lord. The Dark Lord. Yaaaah.
MISTER VOLDY: YES! *Excellent.* The bloodlines of wizard-kind shall be purified. The muddy filth that has latched onto our race will be expunged. And standing upon the precipice, as a shining example of power and might. Will be...*me!* YAAAH!

(He points his wand to the sky. Lightning strikes.)

DEATH BUDDIES: Hahahahaha!
MISTER VOLDY: Now, my Death Buddies. Fetch me my broom.
DEATH BUDDY #1: Oh. Um. We don't need brooms to fly anymore. We just can. *My lord.*
MISTER VOLDY: Good to know. For this information you will be rewarded. With a show of affection. From me.

(Mister Voldy slowly hugs this Death Buddy. He hugs him for a good long while. A hearty hug. The hug ends—Mister Voldy's hands find

their way to the Death Buddy's shoulders. He gives him a nice little neck massage. Mister Voldy works his way down to the Buddy's hand, sensually. Mister Voldy drops to one knee. He gives the hand a nice little kiss. Rest assured, the Death Buddy is horrified by all of this. After far too long of a time, this horror show ends.)

MISTER VOLDY: Everyone *leave*.
DEATH BUDDY #1: Yep.
MISTER VOLDY: *You.* Stay.

(He motions to Xavia. Other Death Buddies exit. Xavia stays.)

MISTER VOLDY: You still wish to go on your *special excursion*?
XAVIA JONES: Yes, my lord.
MISTER VOLDY: You will remain unseen. You will kill anyone who gets in your way.
XAVIA JONES: I will, my lord.
MISTER VOLDY: And if the girl should refuse...
XAVIA JONES: I know what I must do, my lord.
MISTER VOLDY: Yesss. Welcome back...Mrs. Jones. YAH!

(Xavia reveals herself from under her hood. The two laugh and menacingly exit. The Narrator pulls out Book Six.)

NARRATOR: Oh no! It looks like Megan's mother is on a mission in YEAR SIX: PUFFS: THE MUMMY RETURNS!

(The Narrator exits.)

Scene: Snogging 101

The trio enters. They are looking at report cards. Megan and Oliver flirt throughout.

WAYNE HOPKINS: Astronomy.
THE TRIO: Poor.
WAYNE HOPKINS: Herbology.
THE TRIO: Outstanding.
WAYNE HOPKINS: Obviously. Herbology is awesome. ...Defense?
THE TRIO: TROLL.
WAYNE HOPKINS: Yikes.

(A moment of Wayne feeling a bit left out of the group with this new-found romance.)

MEGAN JONES: Wayne, this year we've got to find you a lady friend.
WAYNE HOPKINS: Ha. Yeah. Let's get right on that.
OLIVER RIVERS: You could always date Susie Bones. I hear she's single.

(Susie enters, a mess.)

SUSIE BONES: *My aunt was murdered.* Any second now...*I'll be next.*

(Susie has a moment of crisis. She cries. She laughs. She screams. She exits.)

WAYNE HOPKINS: ...Maybe? Look, as long as the school doesn't become super sexual, I'll be fine...

(The Narrator pops in.)

NARRATOR: How wrong he was!

(Sexy music starts playing. Students enter and sexy dance around Wayne. Even Oliver and Megan get into it.)

NARRATOR: Webster's Dictionary defines snogging as "the act of kissing and caressing amorously—"
WAYNE HOPKINS: —I get it, I get it. Go find a classroom or something.
PUFFS: *Oooo! A classroom!*

(All exit but Megan and Oliver who are still making out.)

WAYNE HOPKINS: HEY!

(Oliver and Megan separate.)

WAYNE HOPKINS: I've been thinking about something else anyway.
MEGAN JONES: What?
WAYNE HOPKINS: Maybe trying out for the sports team.
OLIVER RIVERS: *What?!
MEGAN JONES: *Nooooo!
WAYNE HOPKINS: I'm just thinking about it! I've been so set on doing some sort of big crazy wizard world changing thing that I've never done

any regular teenage stuff. This year? No crazy adventures. No wizard shenanigans. I'm just focusing on dates. And sports!

(An airhorn blows. Various sports players enter with brooms and stand in a tryout line. Zach Smith, a wizard bro, enters.)

ZACH SMITH: Alright, you cocksuckers. Zach Smith here. HEY! FUCK YOU! You knobgobblers wanna play sports? AKA get fuckin' laid?! Cause that's the only reason to play.

(**What follows here can be anything. Literally anything. Any sort of crazy story. A description of a movie plot that Zach Smith experienced. An existential pondering. Just wizard jokes. Just random regular jokes. Often times it is kind of filthy, full of expletives and insults. Sometimes it's kind. What once began as a single line of dialogue transformed into this long, crazy, and fun ride every performance. Nick Carrillo, who originated the role, has improvised a different Zach Smith over 600 times as of this writing, so the sky is the limit. There will be more examples in the back of this script, provided by Nick to give a better idea. Here is my own personal attempt at one. If anything, have fun.)

**Alright, jerk wads. Before we get started, I just have to share something that's been happening to me. Get it off my chest. So. We all know how we can do the spell thing where a glowing little white animal jumps out and scampers around—and those weird security guard dweebs just hate it. They hate those animals. You know, it's supposed to represent something about you—answer a lot of questions. SO. After years of hard work. PRACTICE—WHICH IS IMPORTANT. I finally did it. I did the spell. But my little animal—well, it isn't an animal. Turns out, my special animal thing is a forty-five-year-old accountant named Debra who lives as a single mom in a small town in Oklahoma with two kids. And she is so inconvenienced every time I use that spell. She's just here now, at this secret magic school in Europe. I don't know how to get her back home. So, it turns into a whole—ordeal—she has to book a flight or take a boat. Getting to those is a journey in itself, considering we're in a secret magic school surrounded by magic in the middle of nowhere. I think she's running out of money—which normally she's very good with. I can't help but feel a tiny bit responsible, you know. But—here's where the story takes a twist. I think I'm falling in love with her. I don't know what to do—do I tell her how I feel? I keep bringing her here just to see her, but that just makes her mad. I know I may just be a sixteen-year-old boy who's also a wizard, and she's forty-five, and has her own life—but I think there's really something special there. What do I do? ...What do I do? ...ANYWAY, let's start these tryouts.

(Everyone throws balls for a second. Just an actual second. Zach goes to Wayne.)

ZACH SMITH: Cut it out! Stop! All right. YOINK. Tryouts are over. And guess what. You! You're on the team!

WAYNE HOPKINS: Really?

ZACH SMITH: No. Fuck you. Get out of here. Everyone else. YOU MADE THE TEAM!

EVERYONE ELSE: Really?!

ZACH SMITH: No! FUCK ALL OF YOU! It's a one-man team. ZACH SMITH!

(All exit but Wayne. Sally enters.)

SALLY PERKS: Waaaayne. Hey. I thought you played pretty nice out there.

WAYNE HOPKINS: Oh. Yeah. You know, it's whatever.

SALLY PERKS: Hahaha, I do know. I go to this school. Anyways, cool. Well. Bye.

WAYNE HOPKINS: Wait! Sally. Would you like to...go out on a date sometime?

SALLY PERKS: Sure.

(Sally winks and exits, or at least tries to. Still glasses-less, she cannot find the exit.)

WAYNE HOPKINS: All right! A date. With a girl. Oh no. A date. With a girl!

Scene: Later, in the Hallway

Megan enters, holding a note. She paces. She stops and reads the note. Then paces more.

MEGAN JONES: Ugghhh. Oliver! Where the frigg are you? "Meet at the third-floor corridor formerly out of bounds for anyone who didn't want to die a super painful death." Geez. Remember that? This school. Dangerous for children. Olivvver?

(Xavia enters.)

XAVIA JONES: The boy won't be joining you, I'm afraid.
MEGAN JONES: I'm sorry...who are you?
XAVIA JONES: It's me, Megan. Your mother. Imperion!

(Xavia curses her.)

XAVIA JONES: I think you'll be coming with me, darling. HAHA!

(Xavia exits controlling Megan.)

Scene: Perks of Love

Wayne and Sally run on.

SALLY PERKS: Hahaha! Beat you.
WAYNE HOPKINS: Ha. Yep. You can run just as fast as you said.

(She puckers her lips and stands there.)

WAYNE HOPKINS: What? Oh. Okay.

(He lightly kisses her. She grabs him and really goes for it. Snogging music again.)

WAYNE HOPKINS: Wait! Aren't there, like, security measures against intermingling?
SALLY PERKS: Only in the other houses. They didn't think it was necessary for Puffs. Probably the same reason why we don't even get the Special Teenage Magic Talk.
WAYNE HOPKINS: Wait. Like, Magic Sex-Ed? Who teaches Magic Sex-Ed?

(A Certain Potions Teacher enters.)

A CERTAIN POTIONS TEACHER: And then, the wizard's genitalia, hereby known as the "penis," is then inserted into the witch's "vagina."

(He demonstrates this with his wand and a magic donut. As the wand approaches the donut, he gets a far-away look in his eyes.)

A CERTAIN POTIONS TEACHER: ...Lily.

(A Certain Potions Teacher exits.)

SALLY PERKS: Sooo...want to come upstairs?
WAYNE HOPKINS: Uhhhhhhhhhhh...sure?

(She grabs him, and they run off. The Narrator enters.)

NARRATOR: Oh my. Let's see how Megan and Oliver are faring, shall we? Spoiler alert: much worse.

Scene: Mummy

Oliver and Megan are tied up in a dark room. An ominous tone plays beneath.

OLIVER RIVERS: *AHHHHHHHHHH!
MEGAN JONES: *AHHH!
OLIVER RIVERS: Megan? What's going on?
MEGAN JONES: It's my mom. She's out of Wiz Priz, and she's just as bad-ass as I always believed.
OLIVER RIVERS: I think we're in real danger. She took my wand.

(A scream slowly moves closer in the distance.)

MEGAN JONES: Ooo! She stole my wand too! Awesome.

(A very scared Wayne runs on, screaming.)

WAYNE HOPKINS: AHHH! Hide. Hide! *Hide!*
OLIVER & MEGAN: WAYNE?!
WAYNE HOPKINS: *I'm not running from a sexual experience!* I'm sorry, have I interrupted a weird thing?

(Xavia bursts into the room.)

XAVIA JONES: HAHAHA! Hello, children. Ooh look, another one. Hello there.

(Xavia magics Wayne up against the wall and binds his hands. She pulls Megan down to her.)

XAVIA JONES: Megan, dear. It has been such a long time.
MEGAN JONES: Um. Hi. Uh, Hello. Uh...yes, hi. Wow. Hey. Oh boy. I've dreamed of this moment for like, ever, and *you're actually here* and I'm...hi. I'm Megan. Your daughter and a fan.
XAVIA JONES: Why, thank you. Dear: a thought. Now that I'm free I think it is time I take you far away from here. Just the two of us.
MEGAN JONES: That's...pretty much all I've ever wanted.
XAVIA JONES: Good. But *oh, no.* We have a problem. I've been watching you, Megan. *These two...* are your friends?

(Using magic, she makes them hit themselves.)

WAYNE & OLIVER: Ahh. Why?
XAVIA JONES: I'm disappointed, Megan. *Disappointed* in *you.*
MEGAN JONES: What? What'd I do?
XAVIA JONES: *Nothing*, Megan. You did nothing. I come all this way and what is it I see standing before me? I see *a Puff.*
MEGAN JONES: No.
XAVIA JONES: That's all you are, isn't it?
MEGAN JONES: Stop!
XAVIA JONES: YOU'RE JUST ANOTHER PUFF.
MEGAN JONES: NOOOO!
XAVIA JONES: Yes. You're nothing like me. How disappointing.
MEGAN JONES: I am not a Puff.
XAVIA JONES: Oh? Good. Prove it.

(Xavia magics Oliver and Wayne forward.)

XAVIA JONES: I want you to hurt them. Torture them. *Kill them,* maybe? Prove to me that you are *my daughter.*

(Xavia gives Megan a wand. She points it towards Wayne and Oliver.)

XAVIA JONES: Go on. Do it. And then we can leave. Just us. Just like you've always wanted.

MEGAN JONES: I...

(Megan lowers her wand.)

MEGAN JONES: I won't.
XAVIA JONES: You disappoint me again. *Fine!* YAH!

(Xavia magics the trio to the ground. She hovers over them. Xavia, summoning all of her might, lifts her wand and points it down on them.

XAVIA JONES: *I will do what I must.* Avada...Ke-baba!!!!

(Nothing. The ominous tone disappears. She looks at the wand. She tries again.)

XAVIA JONES: AVADA KEDOOBER. ABRA KADABRABRA. Brahhh. *Braaghh!* No. Hmmmm.

(She practices silently for a moment.)

MEGAN JONES: I'm sorry. Have you done this before?
XAVIA JONES: Oh! *I've done it...maybe.* Don't look at me like that. The Dark Lord himself recruited me! Here, I shall show you that fateful day. Flashbackios! To October 1981!

(We flashback to a dance club. Mister Voldy enters wearing sunglasses. Various Death Buddies enter in '80's gear and dance around the trio. They are having a fun 1980's time. This V.O. can be anyone.)

DJ VOICEOVER (V.O.): It's 1981 and you're at the Dark Lord's Blood Boogie Dance Jam. If you love the Dark Lord...say YEAH.
DEATH BUDDIES: Yeah!

(All keep dancing. Xavia nervously walks up to Mister Voldy and taps him on the shoulder.)

MISTER VOLDY: Yes?
XAVIA JONES: Let me join your evil army? Pleeeeaasssse?
MISTER VOLDY: Fiiine. *Yaaaah!*

(He points his wand at her wrist.)

XAVIA JONES: Wow. Free tattoo! Awesome.

(Time Traveling '80's Zach Smith has entered. [See PUFFS spin off materials, or don't, you'll probably be fine.])

'80s ZACH SMITH: WOAAAH! That lady is EVIIIIL! AND THAT'S WHAT WE SHOULD ALL THINK ABOUT HER.

(He exits.)

MISTER VOLDY: Great! Now, I'm off to kill a baby!
DEATH BUDDIES: Yeaaaah!

(Mister Voldy and Buddies exit.)

XAVIA JONES: Flashback managed.

(Music stops as Death Buddies vanish and everything returns to non-1980's normal.)

XAVIA JONES: See? I'm awesome. Now, AVADA RELEASIO! Oh. Okay.
    So, what I just did was let you go...
MEGAN JONES: Oh. My. Wizard. God. You're just...*you're* just a Puff.
XAVIA JONES: Hi! *Never!*
MEGAN JONES: YOU'RE JUST A PUFF!
XAVIA JONES: No! I. Uh. AVADA KE*[explosion mouth sounds]*! Damnit!
    No. Puffs are lame. Failures! A bunch of dumb, stupid—
WAYNE HOPKINS: FAILURES! ...And *that's* the best thing about being a
    PUFF! Besides being so close to the kitchen.
MEGAN JONES: *Huh?
OLIVER RIVERS: *What?
WAYNE HOPKINS: Follow me here. Puffs are actually awesome and always
    have been. We're the Mighty Ducks of wizards. ...No! The *Mighty
    Ducks 2* of wizards. Cedric knew it, and *maybe even Helga* knew it
    when she was picking students.
OLIVER RIVERS: We never got to finish that story.
WAYNE HOPKINS: Maybe we can now. Asio book! Asio BOOK!

(Wayne holds his wand up. Nothing.)

OLIVER RIVERS: Wayne?
WAYNE HOPKINS: *ASIO BOOK!*

(The Narrator pops out and throws the successfully summoned book to Wayne.)

NARRATOR: Oh, yeah.

WAYNE HOPKINS: Great. "The Tragic Yet Rewarding History of the Puffs." Okay, "The time had come for the founders to choose students..."

(Helga and the Founder puppets enter.)

RIC GRYFF: Students who are brave!

ROWENA: Students whom are smart!

SAL: **Just a bunch of dicks.

> *(**Other solid options here made up by original Sal, Stephen Stout: "Eleven-year-olds with henchmen," "Students who always speak like they are going to throw a glass of white wine in your face" etc. Feel free to find your own.)*

HELGA: Students who are...um. Well...

(Other founders laugh and exit.)

HELGA: I'll take the rest of them. Because as long as they are willing to work hard, everybody should have a place here. Sure, their skill levels will be all over the place, *but that's okay.* There's always a time to improve. This is a school, right? So yes...being brave, or smart, or...snakes, is *great.* But. Why be one thing when you can be...*everything else?* Yes? *Yes.* Now. Where did my cup get off to? Cup? Cup?!

(Helga searches for her cup somewhere off stage.)

WAYNE HOPKINS: So, you see, Megan's mom? You're right. Puffs are failures. We'll try and fight you, and we will probably fail. We'll fail big time. We'll fail so hard—

OLIVER RIVERS: Wayne, I don't know where this is going.

XAVIA JONES: You can't fight me. *I have all these wands.* So meeeeh.

WAYNE HOPKINS: But eventually...we get better. ASIO WAND! WAND!

(The wands fly from her hands into Megan and Oliver's. They point them at Xavia.)

WAYNE HOPKINS: WAND!

(The last wand zooms overhead and embeds itself into the wall. Xavia panics.)

XAVIA JONES: Hey! One of those is mine. No! This can't be happening. You're all just stupid Puffs!
WAYNE HOPKINS: Oh yeah? AVIAFORS!

(A bird appears in Xavia's hand. She screams and throws it off stage.)

MEGAN JONES: Go back to What's-His-Name-That-We-Try-Not-To-Say, Mom. Get out of here.
XAVIA JONES: You have not seen the last of me, children! I will be back!!

(Xavia goes to exit through a door. She has some trouble. Maybe it's locked. Maybe she's just turning it the wrong direction. Eventually, she just leaves through another means. Wayne and Oliver celebrate.)

WAYNE HOPKINS: WE JUST DEFEATED AN EVIL WIZARD!!!
OLIVER RIVERS: YEAH! EVERYONE IS DEFINITELY GONNA HEAR ABOUT THIS!

(Megan does not celebrate.)

WAYNE HOPKINS: Meeeegan? You okay?
MEGAN JONES: That was...a lot to take in.

(Oliver walks over to Megan and hugs her.)

WAYNE HOPKINS: I'm coming in.

(Wayne joins the hug. Like magic, the weird mirror appears behind them.)

WAYNE HOPKINS: Whoa. Weird mirror!
NARRATOR: Yes. The very same mirror stood, its purpose unchanged: to show its onlooker their greatest desire. But that's the funny thing about desires...they change. And whereas once these three saw images of grandeur, or lifelong fantasies...our trio now just saw...this. Three friends. Together.

(The trio smiles for a moment, together. Wayne's reflection then pulls out a lightsaber.)

NARRATOR: And one of them has a lightsaber. Aw.

(The reflection vanishes. The trio pulls out their wands.)

Scene: End of Year Six Where Nothing Major Happens

NARRATOR: Taking their life-threatening experience and true test of friendship to heart, our trio spent the remainder of a relatively calm year to really practice their magic.

WAYNE HOPKINS: Three.

OLIVER RIVERS: Two.

MEGAN JONES: One.

THE TRIO: REPAIRO!

OLIVER RIVERS: Alright, we fixed these glasses I was holding! I think we've done it. We have officially mastered all spells...up to grade three.

WAYNE HOPKINS: Hey, maybe unrelated. But has there always been a giant skull in the sky?

MEGAN JONES: That could mean anything...

(Briefly, a falling sound. It gets louder and louder until a large splat. The trio looks on in horror. Puffs pop out in various places.)

PUFFS: The Headmaster IS DEAD!!!

TRIO: *Fuck.*

(The Narrator enters. The Puffs all assemble and lift up lit wands one by one in solidarity.)

Scene: A Funeral & Instant Messaging

NARRATOR: For some, the death of The Headmaster came as a shock. For others, it was proof that evil had finally triumphed. And for everyone, it meant one very impressively thrown together funeral.

(Somewhere, a phoenix cries. All exit.)

NARRATOR: Summer arrived. Fearing interception of their letters the three decided to try another magical means of communication.

(Something is heard like the "door opening" sound from AOL Instant Messenger. The trio enters in letter writing positions. This time they type on keyboards.)

WAYNE HOPKINS: Hey guys. Thanks for using ***AOL Instant Messenger. I think it will significantly speed up communication. –NotAWizard1997.

OLIVER RIVERS: Good idea. Definitely safer. –MathMagician314159.

MEGAN JONES: What. THE. FUCK. IS. THIS. Ahhh! –PurplePrincess2000.

WAYNE HOPKINS: Ok. Any new updates? I hear things are getting pretty bad out there.

MEGAN JONES: Shit is getting dark. And the rumor is the Ministry is starting to go after Mug Borns.

OLIVER RIVERS: It's true. And it means I won't be going back to school.

WAYNE & MEGAN: What?!

OLIVER RIVERS: I have to go on the run. To protect my family, I wiped their memories. Or, I tried to. I instead turned their heads into oranges. Which will have to do. Megan. You're the world to me. Wayne. You are too. Try not to get into too much trouble.

(The door sound as Oliver exits. After a sad moment, unsure if they'll ever hear from their friend again, Megan and Wayne exit too. The Narrator pulls out Book Seven.)

NARRATOR: YEAR SEVEN! Who lives? Who dies? What crazy new characters join us? Find out in THE FINAL YEAR: THE PUFFS AND THE TIME HARRY CAME BACK AND CAUSED A WAR AT SCHOOL.

(The Narrator exits. Wayne and Megan re-enter, exhausted.)

Scene: The End Begins

MEGAN JONES: So this year's been interesting.

WAYNE HOPKINS: Yeah. They've thrown any attempt at giving us an education out the window. Yesterday in Defense class, they just tortured a kid for three hours.

(A knock at the door. The two pull out their wands, ready for a fight. The door is opened to reveal...nobody. Elsewhere, with much energy, Bippy enters. Bippy is their brand-new elf-helper friend.)

BIPPY: Hello, Mister Wayne Hopkinses! Ms. Megan Joneses! It's me! Bippy! Your little house elf friend.

(**Bippy bursts into a little Bippy song. Feel free to use an option below or make up one of your own. It should be mildly annoying, somewhat adorable, and no more than twenty seconds long, for all our sakes please.)

BIPPY:

(OPTION 1)
I am Bippy, and I am your best friend!
We'll be together 'til the very end!
Bippy! Bippy! We all say: yippeeee!
Did I mention I'm your best friend?!
(Spoken) Verse two of twenty. *(Sung)* I am Bippy—

(OPTION 2)
I am Bippy, and I'm your best friend.
We'll be together 'til the very end!
We're always going on adventures.
You're both wizards and Bippy's indentured.

MEGAN JONES: Bippy! We, uh, have a job for you. We need you to run. Just keep running until we tell you to stop.
BIPPY: Bippy is happy to do it. Magic exit!

(Bippy disappears in the blink of an eye. Or simply runs off stage.)

MEGAN JONES: Oliver is so lucky. He doesn't have to deal with any of this.
WAYNE HOPKINS: Have you heard from him?
MEGAN JONES: No.
WAYNE HOPKINS: I'm sure he's fine.
MEGAN JONES: Yeah.
WAYNE HOPKINS: On the bright side, Potter was the cause of most of our problems, so as long as he stays gone...

(Several Puffs run on.)

HANNAH: Harry's back!

J. FINCH: He's here to start a revolution!
LEANNE: He went camping!
PUFFS: To the Great Hall!

(All find their way to the Great Hall.)

Scene: A Great Hall Again

Harry enters and speaks to the gathered students.

HARRY: Hello! It's me. Harry.
PUFFS: Hi!
HARRY: Oh, how nice. I don't know if any of you remember me. I used to go to school here—aghhh!

(All grab their heads at the sound of feedback, or a megaphone's siren. Mister Voldy appears somewhere. He speaks into a megaphone. All on stage do some really great hearing-a-voice-in-your-head acting.)

MISTER VOLDY: Is this thing on? Your efforts are futile. I do not want to kill you. Give me Potter. And you shall be rewarded. You have until Midnight…night…night…night.

(A moment of silence. Mister Voldy turns to the audience, continuing to talk into the megaphone.)

MISTER VOLDY: That went well, I think. Hmm. So, we've got until midnight. Anyone bring any board games? Or snacks. What do you mean I'm still talking into the megaphone? What? Oh! Bring me Harry...*Harry. Harry*... Okay. The megaphone is now definitely off.

(Then Mister Voldy has SEVERAL OPTIONS. PLEASE CHOOSE ONE:)

MISTER VOLDY:
(OPTION 1): You ever feel like a piece of yourself is missing? I feel like that. Like six or so pieces from right in here are just gone. I can't tell if I'm depressed or my lunch hasn't settled or—ohhhh. I just put something together. What? The megaphone is still on? Really? Oh my. I am just having a day, aren't I? YAH! *Harry!*

81

(OPTION 2): Hmm. Now's as good a time as any to break out my... tight five. Say...have you ever noticed the differences between wizards and witches? Hmm. Tough crowd. That's a "no" on that one. Say—British food. What's the deal with that, huh? It's just so...British. Say. What do all of my enemies have in common? They're all dead. Thank you, that's been my—what? The megaphone is still on? Really? Oh my. I am just having a day, aren't I? YAH! *Harry!*

(OPTION 3): Okay, just a gentle reminder that if I appear to pass out. Don't touch me. Just leave me. I'm fine. Nothing is wrong...I'm just taking a nap. I suddenly got tired and took a nap, right there. I'm not dying—nor is my inability to die at risk—in fact, forget I mentioned this. I want everyone to forget this. What? The megaphone is still on? Really? Oh my. I am just having a day, aren't I? YAH! *Harry!*

(OPTION 4): Now seems like a good time to discuss our plan for what we do AFTER we take over the world of wizards. Let's go over what we've got, write it down if you brought a quill or a pencil. Step one: take over. Step two: Hm. Oh. Nothing. We have nothing planned past that. Anyone have ideas? We can throw a dance or two maybe? Put on my boogie shoes. What? The megaphone is still on? Really? Oh my. I am just having a day, aren't I? YAH! *Harry!*

(OPTION 5): Would anyone like to see some photos from my recent trip to Austria? I killed an old man who was imprisoned. Hahahaha ahhhh. Good times. Fun times. What? The megaphone is still on? Really? Oh my. I am just having a day, aren't I? YAH! *Harry!*

(OPTION 6): Hey! No touching my snake! Don't even think about touching my snake. You look like you're thinking about touching it. Well, don't. Don't even look at it. That's my snake. What? The megaphone is still on? Really? Oh my. I am just having a day, aren't I? YAH! *Harry!*

(OPTION 7): So. Since we're on the verge of our victory to be remembered for all dark ages to come, pats on the back by the way, I've been working on some fun one liners to say when we vanquish our great teenage enemy, Potter. Maybe I can try some out, so you can see how fun they are—eh hem. "Boy who lived? How about the boy who's dead now? HA!" "Nice second scar—the one that's on your whole body—since I killed you." "Mother's love your way out of that!" Or my favorite—"Loser says Avada what—" he says, "What?"—"KEDABRA! "—then he dies. What? The megaphone is still on? Really? Oh my. I am just having a day, aren't I? YAH! *Harry!*

(OPTION 8): I'm going to ask an uncomfortable question right now. I ask for an honest response. Where are my shoes? I've been back three years, and three years—barefooted. No one has offered me a pair of sneakers, or some lounge loafers. Wingtips. At first, I thought oh—maybe this is the fashion—but quickly learned—no—that's not it. One year later, my little piggies are still out for all to see—it became about the principle of the matter—I'm the Dark Lord. Surely someone will offer me some shoes. Or at least ask if I'm comfortable. But now: we are in the woods. We've spent a whole evening outdoors. My feet are wet—I've stepped on several pointy rocks—I may need a tetanus shot. So, no. I am not comfortable. So where are my—what? The megaphone is still on? Really? Oh my. I am just having a day, aren't I? YAH! *Harry!*

(OPTION 9): So. Who's up for some Pilates? Ever since I got this new body—everyone's asked how I keep in such thin shape whilst eating whatever I want. The answer: Pilates. Can't get enough of it. I. The Dark Lord. Love Pilates. My favorite thing about Pilates is that it's building strength and endurance in the whole entire body. I warn you, though—Pilates is not for everyone. But it is for me. I bet if I had done some Pilates before that night seventeen years ago this would be a very different—what? The megaphone is still on? Really? Oh my. I am just having a day, aren't I? YAH! *Harry!*

(After one of those, Mister Voldy exits. Everyone on stage turns and looks at Harry.)

MEGAN JONES: I am having trouble reading the room right now...we want to give him up, right?

(The Narrator jumps in.)

NARRATOR: In that moment, a Snake girl cried out..."GRAB HIM!" And the Puffs reacted accordingly.

(The Puffs form a wall around Harry.)

MEGAN JONES: Okay, I see what we're doing.

NARRATOR: And upon being told to leave the Great Hall for evacuation...it was a Puff who stood up first.

ERNIE MAC: What if we want to stay and fight?

(Everyone mutters, a bit unsure of this course of action.)

WAYNE HOPKINS: Uh, before we rush into anything, can we get just like one minute?

HARRY: Alright. I'm off to find a tiara.

(Harry runs off. If double cast, Susie enters a moment later.)

WAYNE HOPKINS: This is really crazy. People might die. We all might die. Anyone who stays needs to understand that.

HANNAH: But...why would they need us? Everybody says we're the worst at this school.

SALLY PERKS: I don't think they want the stupid people to help fight.

J. FINCH: Yeah. J. Finch is only good at Herbology. Which is the best.

PUFFS: Yeah.

SUSIE BONES: I'll most definitely die if I fight.

MEGAN JONES: It would be easier to just...leave.

(All agree. Slowly, they begin to leave. Even Wayne reluctantly begins to take a step off stage. But—Leanne plants herself firmly center.)

LEANNE: No! I don't want to leave. Why is everyone always so down on us? I won't stand for it anymore! And I won't sit for it either. And I also won't stand on one leg because I can't. Watch. Anyways. Look at your hand! You have a wand!

(Everyone looks at the hand that in fact does not have a wand in it.)

LEANNE: Unless you looked at your other hand. Look at yourselves! Hannah. You used to be so awkward. And you still are, but we don't mind anymore! Who's that? It's Ernie Mac. And he is basically the best. And Sally. Remember that time you did that thing?

SALLY PERKS: I do.

LEANNE: It was amazing! Susie! We all thought you'd be dead by now. But look at you, standing there, alive. Wayne. You give the best hugs. Megan! You give better hugs than you think you do. And J. Finch.

He's imaginary, AND HE CAN DO MAGIC! We all can. We're *wizards*. So, sure. It would be easy to leave. But wouldn't it be wrong? We should do what's right. Like Cedric. I'm a Puff and I'm staying, because if we don't fight now we may never find out how that hat talks!

(Leanne puts her wand center. All others join her with their own, one by one.)

HANNAH: I'm a Puff. And I'm staying.
J. FINCH: I'm a Puff. And I'm staying.
SUSIE, SALLY, & ERNIE: I'm a Puff. I'm staying.
MEGAN JONES: We might die. Are we all willing to die for Harry?
WAYNE HOPKINS: We won't die for Harry. We'll die for each other. I'm a Puff. I'm staying.

(All look to Megan. Slowly, she joins.)

MEGAN JONES: ...I'll stay.

(She puts her wand in, but all others take theirs out. Not good enough, they give her a judging look.)

MEGAN JONES: And I'm a Puff. I'm a Puff.

(No one puts their wands back in yet. They want her to go deeper into her soul.)

MEGAN JONES: Look. my socks don't match. I struggle with reading. I was secretly a member of the Frog Choir. I'm a Puff!

(Everyone puts their wand in and waves.)

PUFFS: Hi!
MEGAN JONES: HIIIIIIIIIIIII!
WAYNE HOPKINS: Alright, if we're going to fight alongside the Braves and the Smarts and not the Snakes, since they've been officially acknowledged as evil, we sure as hell better make sure we take down more bad guys than them.
ERNIE MAC: So then, third or nothing?
WAYNE HOPKINS: No. First or nothing.
PUFFS: *FIRST OR NOTHING!*

(All lift their wands as the battle begins.)

Scene: The Battle

Music! The battle is a lot of running around and entering from various spots to replicate the large-scale war at the school. On top of their own characters, all play Death Buddies too. The music should bounce between an epic war score and an homage to the sweet hits of the 1990's. Sometimes it would like to be both. As it begins, all others rush off leaving Hannah alone on stage, unsure what to do. A Death Buddy pops out and fires two spells that Hannah blocks. A third spell knocks her to the ground. The Death Buddy raises their wand.

HANNAH: Wait! Wait! I give up.

(The Death Buddy laughs and turns to leave. Hannah lifts her wand and does a spell.)

HANNAH: JIGGLY LEGS!! Ha! Get it? I was bullying you!

(The Death Buddy is knocked off stage. Hannah exits as Wayne enters. He fires spells at an unseen assailant.)

WAYNE HOPKINS: Puff on this!

(Susie passes Wayne, pursued by a Death Buddy. They exit. Wayne looks to where they ran off.)

WAYNE HOPKINS: ...Yipee kiyay, mother-Puffer!

(Wayne flips his wand, fires a spell and chases them off. Leanne enters with Sally riding on her back. Sally shoots spells.)

SALLY PERKS: Rickmansempra! Locomotor Legs! Tarantula Jelly!

(They exit. J. Finch runs on screaming, chased by Death Buddies.)

J. FINCH: AHHHHHHHHHHHHHHHHHHHHHHHHHHHHHHHHHHHHHHH!

(A Scooby-Doo-esque chase scene through various doors. Eventually, after a comical number of doors have been entered and exited, they stop.

Harry enters and puts on his new-found tiara. He dances. He exits.

J. Finch and the Death Buddies all emerge at once. J. Finch retreats, as the Death Buddies gather around where they last saw him. Instead of finding J. Finch—they find ZACH SMITH. Death Buddies run as he shoots spells.)

ZACH SMITH: Fuck you! Fuck you! Zach Smith came back to school. Zach Smith *came!*

(Zach exits. Wayne and Megan enter, ducking and walking carefully. A Death Buddy rushes on and swings a spell at them. They dodge it as the Death Buddy flees. They look off after them.)

WAYNE HOPKINS: Gah. If only we could hit them from this distance.
MEGAN JONES: It's impossible. You would have to know the exact angle to aim your wand. There's no way to figure that out.

(Oliver Rivers, tattered, dirty, and bloodied, bursts in.)

OLIVER RIVERS: Sounds like you could use a protractor.
MEGAN JONES: Oliver?!

(Megan and Wayne run to him. All hug.)

OLIVER RIVERS: I heard about the battle. There are so many secret passages into this school. It's dangerous for children. But! You need to hit those people way out there? Time to see a REAL math magician at work!

(Dramatic music and just epic stuff as Oliver maths. He maths hard. Harder than anyone ever mathed.)

MEGAN JONES: How's that coming along? Because quickly would be great.

(Oliver positions Wayne's wand accordingly.)

OLIVER RIVERS: Left a little. Right. Left. There. You're good to go.

WAYNE HOPKINS: EAT SLUGS!

(A beat. Then a vomiting sound from that direction.)

OLIVER & MEGAN: Nice.

(Xavia dramatically enters. A shift in music/lights. A signal that a maybe epic showdown will take place.)

XAVIA JONES: Yes, very nice. Hello, children.
MEGAN JONES: You two go. I'll handle this.

(Wayne and Oliver nod to each other and quickly exit. Megan and Xavia assume dueling poses.)

MEGAN JONES: Hello, Mom.
XAVIA JONES: Megan, I'm not here for pleasantries. I'm just here to finish unfinished business. Haha! AVADA SKADOO! *Damnit.*
MEGAN JONES: Okay, seriously?! It's two words. Avada. Kedabra. Avada Kedabra. It's simple.
XAVIA JONES: Oh, is it?! Is it simple...WELL...

(A Death Buddy wanders on. He's distracted, thinking about his family.)

XAVIA JONES: AVADA KEDABRA!

(A flash of green light. The Death Buddy drops motionless to the ground, dead. Xavia takes a second to process.)

XAVIA JONES: AHHHHH! OH MY WIZARD GOD. It's...it's that easy?! WHY IS IT SO EASY?! You say two words, and then they just...okay. I'm okay.

(Another random Death Buddy enters and goes to his dead Death Buddy friend. He lifts the body up and carries it off stage.)

RANDOM DEATH BUDDY: Someone has to tell his evil wife and kids.
XAVIA JONES: Ohhh, now it feels worse.
MEGAN JONES: Mom. That's what all of your "friends" do. To everyone.
XAVIA JONES: I don't like the way it feels. I...oh god. I'm a Puff. I get it. I'm a Puff! Oh! Who would have thought the people in the hoods and

the masks would be so in the wrong? ...Fine. Do it. Kill me! THE FATE A MURDERER DESERVES.

(Xavia holds Megan's wand to her head.)

MEGAN JONES: Yeah, so, considering the one person you've killed was evil...I don't think you'll get in too much trouble? Just say you were a secret spy or something?
XAVIA JONES: Oh...

(Xavia hugs Megan. A Death Buddy enters, poised to attack. They stop upon seeing this beautiful family moment.)

DEATH BUDDY: Aww.
MEGAN JONES: *Stupidfy!
XAVIA JONES: *Avada Kedabra!

(A flash of green light. The Death Buddy is stunned, knocked away, and also dead.)

MEGAN JONES: *Mom!*

(Xavia hands Megan her wand.)

XAVIA JONES: Here, you take this. If we make it out of here, I owe you so many birthday presents.

(The two exit as battle music returns. Ernie and J. Finch enter. Ernie fires many spells at Death Buddies seen and unseen. J. Finch just sort of dodges and rolls around. A pause in the action.)

ERNIE MAC: So—if you're imaginary, how come the bad people can see you?

(Ernie fires more spells around the room.)

J. FINCH: They must have special glasses!
ERNIE MAC: Then how come I can see you?
J. FINCH: ...You must be special.

(A Death Buddy jumps on ready to attack.)

ERNIE & J. FINCH: *STUPIDFY! *AHHH!

(The Death Buddy falls backwards.)

J. FINCH: Looks like he ordered a side of Mac & Finch.

(Ernie and J. Finch exit, holding hands. Harry, the little scamp, enters, carrying Ron Mop and a Hermeoone Wig. They casually walk through the carnage of the battle as a Death Buddy chases them. The Death Buddy fires several spells at the three. They miss. They miss again. They miss again. Harry smiles and exits. The Death Buddy curses the wizard gods above. They exit.

Wayne runs on. He stops dead in his tracks. A giant unseen creature blocks his path.)

WAYNE HOPKINS: Puffs Emergency Formation #10!

(The Puffs rush in and gather around Wayne. In slow motion—and to music—all shoot a spell together at the creature. The Puffs, all together, are winning. Nothing could possibly go wrong now, not when they are together. Perhaps we even get a glimpse of Wayne's "Expectation Animal," a whale. The creature is defeated as everyone celebrates. It's cut short as the castle quakes. All scream in terror and split up—leaving Megan and Sally Perks. The two meet in the middle, back-to-back.)

MEGAN JONES: You okay?
SALLY PERKS: I think so...ohhhhh, fine.

(Sally Perks, after years of most things being blurry, puts her glasses on.)

SALLY PERKS: There. Sally Perks is suited up and ready to kick some—

(A Death Buddy enters.)

DEATH BUDDY: AVADA KEDABRA!

(A flash of green light. Sally instantly falls into Megan's arms, dead. Stunned, Megan carries her away. The tone shifts to something more serious, as Susie runs on out of breath. She wonders if death has finally found her. A giant spider blocks her path.)

SUSIE BONES: Extermios!

(The spider leaves in pain. Susie runs to a door. A Death Buddy stands ready to attack, but Susie beats them to the punch with a spell of her own.)

SUSIE BONES: EXISTENTIO CRISIS! *Not today!*

(She slams the door as Ernie runs on.)

ERNIE MAC: Susie! Quick! There's too many of them. We're regrouping in the common room.

(Susie runs ahead. Behind her, Ernie is stopped and frozen by a few spells from a Death Buddy. They lift their wand.)

DEATH BUDDY: AVADA—

(J. Finch runs on and dives between Ernie and the Death Buddy.)

J. FINCH: No!
DEATH BUDDY: —KEDABRA!

*(A flash of green light. J. Finch falls into Ernie Mac, dead. Ernie Mac takes out the Death Buddy with a spell of his own.
Megan, Wayne, Oliver, and Susie enter. They see J. Finch. They realize Sally is not there either.)*

WAYNE HOPKINS: They're everywhere. Spread out, head to the basement! And stay alive.

(All exit. J. Finch's wand remains on stage. A moment of stillness. Leanne jumps on. She looks around, confused. She finds J. Finch's wand and picks it up.)

LEANNE: Hello? Where'd everybody go? Did we win?

(Epic battle music. Slowly, from every possible direction, as many Death Buddies as possible enter. They laugh and surround Leanne. A simple task for these Death Buddies. All seems lost.

Leanne lifts up both the wands she holds. She takes out several of the Death Buddies immediately. Then more. A flurry of spells, as the fighting intensifies. She summons a teddy bear to take out a Death Buddy who struggles in the background. The Death Buddies swirl around her as she fights them all with ease. She spins. She flips. She knocks out more. She sends two others to the ground behind her. She's won. A cheer of triumph. Not only that—she looks down to find she has ended the fight standing on one leg.)

LEANNE: I did it!

(Death Buddies enter behind her. They point their wands.)

DEATH BUDDIES: AVADA KEDABRA.

(A flash of green light. Leanne falls to the ground, dead.

Wayne, Oliver, and Megan enter exhausted. A Death Buddy sneaks up behind them, ready to kill.)

WAYNE HOPKINS: It's okay. I think it's almost over. We just need to hold out a little longer.

(Bippy enters and spots the Death Buddy.)

BIPPY: NO! You will not hurt Megan Joneses!!

(Bippy stops the Death Buddy in midair with her magic. The Death Buddy swings his wand.)

DEATH BUDDY: SLASHIOS!

(The Death Buddy runs off—Bippy grasps her throat. She knows it's her end. Her life flashes before her eyes, and she realllly takes her time dying.)

BIPPY: Bippy has done a good job, yes? I am forever grateful for all of the time we spent together...just remember Bippy as someone who's been here *this whole time.* I was Bippy...*I was...*

(Bippy falls to the ground, dead. A pause as the trio takes in this moment.)

OLIVER RIVERS: Who the fuck was that?

(The three step over Bippy's corpse. They look at the carnage in front of them.)

WAYNE HOPKINS: Guys. This...this is crazy.
MEGAN JONES: We are fighting in a war.
OLIVER RIVERS: This is a lot for eighteen-year-olds to handle.
WAYNE HOPKINS: Is this how Potter feels all the time?
THE TRIO: It suuucks.

(Harry runs on, pursued by Death Buddies.)

HARRY: Oh, *EXCUSE ME!*

(Harry pushes past Wayne and exits. A Death Buddy sends a spell at Harry but misses his mark.)

DEATH BUDDY: AVADA KEDABRA!

(Everything goes green. For a moment, nothing.

Wayne falls to the ground. Dead.)

OLIVER & MEGAN: Wayne?!

(Blackout.)

Scene: A Very White Room

Lights up on a bright white room. The Second Headmaster stands waiting. Wayne jumps up, terrified and confused.

WAYNE HOPKINS: AHHHHHHH!! What? Where? Where am I?

(The Second Headmaster turns and is surprised to find this other student here.)

SECOND HEADMASTER: ...You—are not Harry. Umm...I want to say *Wayne?*
WAYNE HOPKINS: Headmaster? But you're...am I?
SECOND HEADMASTER: I'm afraid that must be the case.

WAYNE HOPKINS: Oh.

(Wayne tries to let this sink in. He looks around.)

WAYNE HOPKINS: Where are we?

SECOND HEADMASTER: To be honest I'm not sure. It's more of a thing for Harry.

WAYNE HOPKINS: Of course it is. Headmaster...this...this seems really unfair. I just watched my friends die. And now me? What was the point? I won't be remembered for anything. No one will know my name. I'm just some...unnamed dead kid in a school battle. *Potter's* battle. He gets to be the hero. He gets to be everything I ever wanted. Why did I have to be so...unimportant?

SECOND HEADMASTER: Wayne, it is very easy to feel like you're only a secondary character in someone else's grand story. That does not mean, however, there isn't another story out there that's all about you. The one where you're the most important person in the world. The hero. We're all important, Wayne. And we're all unimportant. We're all heroes. In some way. To someone. And as for your story? I think it was pretty cool.

WAYNE HOPKINS: So...there's not some big surprise and I'll open my eyes right where I died?

SECOND HEADMASTER: I'm afraid not.

WAYNE HOPKINS: But I was finally good at magic.

SECOND HEADMASTER: There's only one magic we ever really need, Wayne. A magic that will let you live on. The greatest magic there is. Love. And on that note. I really *hate* to do this but...I am expecting someone...and so...uh...

WAYNE HOPKINS: Oh. ...Yeah.

(Wayne starts to exit. He turns.)

WAYNE HOPKINS: Headmaster. Just one more thing. Did I really spend seven years at wizard school to find out that you believe love is the greatest magic there is?

SECOND HEADMASTER: ...Yes...see for yourself.

(The Second Headmaster motions to Wayne. Checking his pockets, Wayne finds the special Puff item he and his fellow classmates were given after being sorted way back in year one. He holds it tight and lightly smiles.)

WAYNE HOPKINS: ...Okay.

(Wayne exits. A silent moment. Then Harry bursts in.)

HARRY: Woooow! A train station! *(Gasp)* Oh, I'm dead.

(Harry then sees and runs to hug The Second Headmaster, excited. Blackout. The Narrator enters.)

NARRATOR: And that is how Wayne Hopkins, student, died. You probably know the rest of the story. The "boy who lived" lived again. He vanquished evil...

(Harry and Mister Voldy pop out. Harry shoots a spell. Mister Voldy is vanquished.)

HARRY: Expellidermis!
MISTER VOLDY: Nooo.

(They are gone.)

NARRATOR: But now...you at least know a slightly different story. The Story of the Puffs. You know, I think eventually we all find that little part of us. The Puff. Maybe it's there in the moments where you lose your keys. Or momentarily forget how old you are. Or maybe it's that part of you that works hard, the part that remains loyal and true despite whatever terrifying monsters are thrown your way. The part that plays fair, even when life is *anything but.* Maybe that's a Puff there. Now, one last question. Where do I fit in to all of this? You'll get that answer in our obligatory segment: NINETEEN YEARS LATER!

Scene: Nineteen Years Blah, Blah. An Epilogue.

The platform of a train station. An older Megan Jones stands waiting. Blondo crosses with his own child, Scorpy.

BLONDO: Now, remember. What's our NUMBER ONE rule?
BLONDY & SCORPY: *No time travel.*
BLONDO: That's my boy...*young Scorpius.*

(Blondo and Scorpy exit. CAPE TWIRL! Oliver enters.)

OLIVER RIVERS: Holy shit, Megan. You are never gonna believe what Potter named his new kid!

MEGAN JONES: Wait! Where's Wayne?

OLIVER RIVERS: I thought you had him.

MEGAN JONES: Oh fuck, not this again. Did we leave him at my mom's?! WAYNE? Wayne?!

WAYNE RIVERS-JONES (O.S.): Mom! DAD!

(The Narrator, now an eleven-year-old child, runs on. This is Wayne Rivers-Jones.)

WAYNE RIVERS-JONES: Mom. Dad. I'm scared to go to school.

MEGAN JONES: I'll be honest with you, Wayne. You should be. When I was there: if it wasn't an evil teacher, it was a giant snake. Or Soul Sucking Security Guards. One year there was a sports tournament. *Someone died.* You'll be fine. Just remember: through it all. No matter if you're Brave, or Smart, or *[** REPEAT what SAL said in Year Six about Snakes]*, or: a Puff. Don't worry too much about it. It's just what some hat thinks.

OLIVER RIVERS: And hey, Wayne: what's three times four?

WAYNE RIVERS-JONES: I don't know.

OLIVER RIVERS: Yep. Well. Don't worry about that either. There's no math class! Still not bitter about that! Just worry about the wizard-ing.

WAYNE RIVERS-JONES: But...what if I'm bad at being a wizard?

OLIVER RIVERS: Son. You are named after someone who started out as one of the worst wizards ever. ...Now, you've got a train to catch.

NARRATOR: I like trains!

(Megan kisses them on the cheek as they rush off. Megan and Oliver watch them go.)

OLIVER RIVERS: You ready for this? New kid's name: Albus Severus.

MEGAN JONES: I can beat it. Scorpius.

OLIVER RIVERS: No! Man. These people have no idea how to name children. By the way did you see Potter? That new job has him really overworked. I feel bad for the guy. Him and his family. It's like he's cursed. It's like they're all...*Cursed Children.*

MEGAN JONES: ...What are you talking about?

OLIVER RIVERS: I don't know, I'm tired. ...Hey. What house do you think he'll get sorted into?

MEGAN JONES: I have a pretty good idea.

(They exit. We shift back to magic school once more as an elderly Professor McG places a stool center with a magic hat on it.

The Narrator slowly enters, dressed in standard wizard robes. They shyly walk to the stool and sit down. The magic talking hat finds its way to their head. They take a nervous breath. They smile. All is fine. Blackout.

The End.)

The Narrator

The Narrator is a role with no specific gender, save for the epilogue scene. While the original actor in the role was male, it has not always been so. Should the Narrator of a production be a female identifying actor, I offer these three slightest of changes to the last scene of the play.

First: Change all usages of the name "Wayne" to "Wayna."

Second: Change "Oh, son" to "Hey."

Third: Add the following bit into the dialogue:

OLIVER RIVERS: No! Man. These people have no idea how to name children.

>   *(A pause. Oliver and Megan have a brief moment of questioning and realization.)*

OLIVER & MEGAN: *Wayna.*

>   *(They shrug it off.)*

OLIVER RIVERS: By the way did you see Potter? That new job really has him overworked. I feel bad for the guy. Him and his family. It's like he's cursed. It's like they're all...*Cursed Children.*

And that's all to change, and only if you want to. Also, to anyone whose name is actually Wayna: I actually quite like the name, and please take no offense.

Puffs: A History

Like nearly all artistic endeavors, *Puffs* changed dramatically from its initial reading to where it landed several years later Off-Broadway. We thought it'd be fun to let you take a peek at some of what *could* have been, what *was* for a brief period of time, and *why* these changed. This is only the tiniest look, as the amount of cut pages would probably be longer than this whole book. The first reading of the show was close to two hours long. (For instance, there was once an entire plot involving Helga's magic box of magic which the Puffs used to save the day.) These were some of my favorites.

An Alternate Introduction

While the original reading still opened as we open today—"Heroes. Made. Not—etc." There was a brief moment where the show began with a scene of Wayne's journey on a certain train. This introduced us immediately to our Puff hero, Wayne, and in a sense, transported the audience to A Certain School of Magic and Magic via a familiar means of getting there. Ultimately, the Narrator introduction would still need to come after this in terms of information, and all of a sudden no one was sorted for ten minutes, so it went away. However, the line "wizard school is just like regular school" stuck with me, and I knew I had to find a place for it later.

> *The sound of a train whistle followed by the rumblings of that very same train. Lights come up on a train car full of ten-year-old children/new wizards: Wayne Hopkins, Leanne, Seamus, and Mandy.*

WAYNE HOPKINS: So...getting into that train station was confusing, right?

(Everyone sort of smiles and nods and looks away.)

WAYNE HOPKINS: I thought the weird platform name was just a British thing. ...I've never been to England before, so I just thought it was British. ...It's not. ...I don't know anyone in England. I've never been a wizard before. *[Pause]* Walking through a wall was pretty cool though.
SEAMUS: Oy. All a part of going to magic school.
WAYNE HOPKINS: Yeah. I guess we're all wizards right?

MANDY: Yes. We're all wizards. We wouldn't be on a train going to a wizard school if we weren't all witches or wizards. My God. Shut up.

LEANNE: I like trains. You get on it in one place, and then you get off in a different place.

MANDY: Ugh. I should have gone to the school in France.

(Megan Jones enters. She points at an open seat next to Wayne.)

MEGAN JONES: Anyone sitting there?

MANDY: Yes. *Yes someone is.* Right, Wayne? RIGHT?

MEGAN JONES: Ah. I get it. Really nice. I'll remember this. *WAYNE.*

(Megan gives them a very evil eye. Maybe she points.)

MANDY: Oh dear. You're on her bad side now. I can't believe they even let her come to school.

SEAMUS: What do you mean?

MANDY: That girl's mum...she was one of the darkest witches ever. She worked for...You Know Who.

WAYNE HOPKINS: ...Who?

MANDY: You know. He-Whose-Name-We-Can't-Say.

WAYNE HOPKINS: ...What are you talking about?

MANDY: Thou-Whose-Nameth-We-Musn't-Ever-Speaketh—never mind he was an evil wizard.

WAYNE HOPKINS: *(Gasp)* There are evil wizards?

MANDY: Yes. And they say she's the next one. And they say her mum taught her everything she knows. *And you're on her bad side.*

WAYNE HOPKINS: Oh. My God.

(An awkward, frightful silence.)

SEAMUS: What house do you reckon you'll be sorted in, hm?

MANDY: I'm very smart. So probably the Smarts. But, I wouldn't mind being a Brave or a Silver Snake. The cool kids always end up in one of those. It's the other one I'm worried about. Ugh. I would probably just leave.

LEANNE: *Look! A castle!*

(Everyone gets up to look out the window.)

WAYNE HOPKINS: Wow.

SEAMUS: Oy! We'd best get in our robes!

WAYNE HOPKINS: Wait! One quick question. So, when we say we can do magic do we mean like Willow or like Narnia...or like *Doctor Strange* magic?

MANDY: Ugh. I can't. I'm changing in a different car.

SEAMUS: Oy! I'll come with you!

(They leave. It's just Leanne and Wayne. Leanne stops looking out the window.)

LEANNE: Where did everyone go?

WAYNE HOPKINS: I think I scared them off...

LEANNE: Oh. AHH!

(She runs out the car in terror.)

WAYNE HOPKINS: Great...wizard school is just like regular school...

(A Very Tall Man pops his head in.)

A VERY TALL MAN: Come on then. Off the train!

WAYNE HOPKINS: AHHHHH!

(He runs away as a strange British man in a suit holding some books enters.)

NARRATOR: Heroes: made. Not born. Except when sometimes they are born.

Free Willy Monologue

In terms of sheer iterations, this probably changed the most. Every rehearsal included an apology to original Wayne actor, Zac Moon, that there was in fact a new version of the *Free Willy* monologue. There are even multiple emails I found while looking for these within previews where it changed, was cut, was added back in, was cut again, was brought back but shorter, and more.

I always knew some version of this would be in the script though, as I love how rooted in the 1990's a *Free Willy* reference is. I loved the feeling that hearing someone mention *Free Willy* gave me. I loved that it fit perfectly in the timeline. And I loved the idea that Wayne is so rooted in pop culture, that he can find so much meaning in everyone's favorite *let's free this whale* movie.

Here are a few different versions of it.

WAYNE HOPKINS: Dear Oliver & Megan. So, a movie just came out. Megan, movies are like wizard photographs, but better. It was called *Free Willy*. It's about a group of three friends and this super rude whale. But the whale, he's actually a great whale. So, the three friends work together, and they free the whale and he jumps over this rock and suddenly everyone's like '"WOW! He WAS a great whale."' I guess I've just been thinking maybe the Puffs are the whale and we're the three friends who are destined to bring it to greatness? –Wayne. P.S. HOW DOES THIS OWL KNOW WHERE TO GO?!

WAYNE HOPKINS: Dear Oliver & Megan. So, a movie just came out. Megan, movies are like wizard photographs, but with a plot and production value, and just way better. It's called *Free Willy*. It's about a group of three friends and this super rude whale. But, you see...the whale is actually a great whale. So the three friends work together and they free the whale and he jumps over this rock and suddenly everyone's like '"WOW! Those kids were right. He WAS a great whale."' And I've just been thinking maybe the Puffs are the whale and we're the three friends who are destined to help it jump over that rock and into history as the best house ever? I think so. –Wayne. P.S. HOW DOES THIS OWL KNOW WHERE TO GO?!

WAYNE HOPKINS: Dear Megan & Oliver. A movie just came out. It's called *Free Willy*. It's about this boy and a super rude whale. But, you see...the whale is actually a great whale. So the boy and his two new friends take on this evil amusement park owner and his insurance fraud scheme. Eventually, they free the whale, he jumps over a rock, and suddenly everyone's like 'WOW! He really WAS a great whale.' It was amazing. And I've just been thinking about my wizard destiny and maybe...maybe...the Puffs are that misunderstood whale, and it's not just me who has to do something amazing for them, but it's me and my two friends? Be on the ready for adventure this year. It's definitely coming. –Wayne. P.S. HOW DOES THIS OWL KNOW WHERE TO GO?!

Xavia Jones—Misunderstood Secret Spy Good Person

While *Free Willy* had the most iterations, what changed the most from the PIT to Off-Broadway was Megan and Xavia Jones. Megan initially kept her more goth-inspired attitude all throughout the play. It wasn't until the move where we found her yearly re-inventions of identity as a key part of her character (and a way of exploring the personality dynamics of the school). To match all of the re-writes done there, Xavia's entire plot changed as well. Originally, she was just a full Puff the whole time—and everything about being evil was all a misunderstanding. While funny, it did deflate some of the drama too late in the play. Eventually, Xavia morphed into a true villain—but this being Puffs—a Puff-y villain. Here's what her scene with the trio in Year Six originally looked like, as well as a moment a bit later on.

Xavia bursts into the room.

XAVIA JONES: You will stay right here. Nobody LEAVES! LIGHTSWITCHIOS!

(Xavia does some sort of magic and the lights go completely out.)

OLIVER RIVERS: AHH! Wayne! Do something.
WAYNE HOPKINS: Ah! Ah! Lumos!

(Nothing.)

OLIVER RIVERS: Wayne that is a year one spell.
WAYNE HOPKINS: Well, I…AH! AH! SHE'S GOT ME!!! AHHHHHHH!
MEGAN JONES: Wayne?! MOM! Please. Don't hurt him.

(A beat of silence... then.)

XAVIA JONES: AVADA KEDABRA!

(A flash of green light.)

MEGAN JONES: *AHHHHHH!
OLIVER RIVERS: *...Wayne?!
XAVIA JONES: It's dead. LUMOS!

(The stage lights up. Wayne is crouching. Wayne holds the spider? Maybe?)

XAVIA JONES: I got it. The Scary Spider. Now then...to deal with *you.*

WAYNE HOPKINS: Please don't kill me. Or Oliver. Or Megan. Please? PLEASE?!

XAVIA JONES: Oh, I will...what? I'm not here to kill Megan. Or anyone!

WAYNE HOPKINS: *What?

OLIVER RIVERS: *Huh?

MEGAN JONES: *What now?

XAVIA JONES: The first thing I told you when I walked into this room was that everything you've heard about me is a misunderstanding. I explained my situation, and I didn't act strangely, or make any mysterious threats, right?

OLIVER RIVERS: You did the opposite of all of that.

XAVIA JONES: Oh! Sorry. I tell you, we adults can be forgetful sometimes. And oh no. I even tied you up. I'm sorry. Here's your wands.

MEGAN JONES: What's going on? Is this an evil mom trick?

XAVIA JONES: Children. I have been sent here on a secret mission by the Dark Lord himself. But...I have betrayed him.

WAYNE HOPKINS: What mission?

XAVIA JONES: To infiltrate your student body as an average fifteen-year-old. To build up trust amongst the staff and fellow students, maybe finally have my first kiss, and finally...assist another student in *the murder of The Headmaster!* Don't worry. He has been warned. Definitely something wrong with his hand though.

(And then she left amicably. Later in the play—upon the trio discussing via AOL instant messenger what their plans for the next year were, Xavia joined in too.)

XAVIA JONES: Hi. I've found a place to lie low. It's called a Howard Johnson's. It's magical. Yet, I fear I have been discovered. Also, more bad news. The Dark Lord will be taking over the school. Mug Borns will not be safe to return. Oliver, you must go into hiding. I recommend Howard Johnson's. For you others, I believe it will still be the safest place you can be. Megan dear, I'm sorry I couldn't be there more for you. Good luck.

(She then was murdered and was gone forever.)

Detective Leanne

One of the best lessons a writer will learn is to "kill your darlings." Getting rid of story beats or characters that don't necessarily advance things forward. What follows is still an idea I am sad never found its way into the show past the first readings. Leanne as the only person who knows something is wrong in Year Four made all the sense in the world, and led to some fun genre shenanigans. But, Year Four is already the longest chunk of the play, and it had to go. (My apologies to original Leanne actor, Andy Miller.) But I am happy for it to see the light of day now.

REAL MR. MOODY: We call it THE GREEN LIGHT CURSE. Because when you use it. There's a bright. Green. Light.

(He does the spell. There's a bright green light.)

ALL: Ahhh!
REAL MR. MOODY: Now, who wants to see me mess with some spiders?

(Leanne's hand shoots up.)

LEANNE: Mr. Moody, I just wanted to say I am your biggest fan. I've read all about you and I hang a picture of you over my bed, and over all the pictures of my family in my house, and in paintings—and if you're here now how are you there—anyways I met you when I was four and you said if I ever saw you again to say this to you:..."Sneaker Beakers."

(She smiles big with anticipation.)

REAL MR. MOODY: Right. Everyone follow me so I can use illegal spells on you.

(All exit except Leanne, whose smile fades.)

LEANNE: He didn't remember me. I've waited for so long but—but. Wait a second.

(She calculates, AKA swivels her head back and forth.)

LEANNE: GASP! That's not the real Mr. Moody! But then...where *is* the real

Moody?

(She pulls out a magnifying glass.)

LEANNE: *Leanne is on the case.*

(She uses the magnifying glass on everything as she exits.)

LATER:

Leanne enters as Wayne, Megan, and Oliver ponder dates.

LEANNE: *It's someone with the name....Jr.*
OLIVER: Leanne! Wayne here has a question.
LEANNE: A question, what's that?!

LATER:

After the Second Task and everyone has run off to study.

NARRATOR: With the Third Task months away, the school became somewhat focused on *education.* Except one girl—whose quest for the truth culminated in several shocking surprises.

(Leanne enters in a trench coat and a fedora—she stands beneath moonlight. Mystery music plays.)

LEANNE: Perhaps it was the cool night air that brought on the chill up my spine. Or perhaps it was merely...knowledge. Truth. For the truth was mine alone to have. Real Mr. Moody was an imposter. This vial of unused potion proves it. But who? Who you ask would do such a thing? Someone at the Ministry. Someone with an evil and slightly convoluted agenda. Someone like supposedly deceased criminal BARY JR. The perfect crime—he thought no one could stop him. But he never counted on LEANNE taking up the case. WAIT TIL I TELL EVERYONE! HIGH FIVE!

(She misses high fiving herself and slaps her own head very hard.)

LEANNE: Hmm...I can't remember a thing.

(She exits singing.)

Enter Mister Voldy

This one isn't entirely different than what ultimately found its way in the show, but there are two jokes here that I just still find funny and thought someone should see them. Those being, Mister Voldy forgetting his keys, and *"Loser says Avada what?"*

Death Buddies flood the stage, standing menacingly.

NARRATOR: The World of Wizards was changing. No one was safe. Wandmakers. Bridges. No one. For evil stood at the door. And he was knocking.

(A knock at a door behind the Death Buddies.)

MISTER VOLDY: Excuse me! I seem to have misplaced my keys.

(A Death Buddy opens the door and Mister Voldy surges in.)

MISTER VOLDY: YES! *Excellent.* The bloodlines of wizard-kind shall be purified. The muddy filth that has latched onto our race will be exterminated. A new dawn is rising. The natural order shall be restored. And standing upon the precipice, as an example of power and might. Will be me!

(He points his wand up. Lightning. Laughter. What fun. A Death Buddy raises his hand.)

MISTER VOLDY: Fetch me my broom.
DEATH BUDDY #1: We don't need brooms to fly anymore. You just can. My lord.
MISTER VOLDY: Good to know. For this information you will be rewarded. With a show of affection. From me.

(Mister Voldy hugs him very awkwardly and for a long time.)

MISTER VOLDY: Now. Loser says Avada what-

DEATH BUDDY #1: Avada what?
MISTER VOLDY: KEDABRA!

(Death Buddy #1 falls to the ground, dead.)

MISTER VOLDY: Everyone. Leave. You. *Stay.*

Extra Zach Smiths

Hey everybody, Nick Carrillo here! I am the actor who originated the J. Finch/Others role, which of course includes Zach Smith. Over the years I had the honor and task of improvising a different scene for that character every night. As I am writing this, I'm about to leave the show and have done over 600 different Zach Smiths. The production team has kindly asked me to contribute a few of my favorites to the script. As you'll see they tend to devolve into non-canon stuff. I always enjoyed taking ideas from pop culture, something that happened in the world that day, or even things that happened to me. Also, I played the role pretty crude, so that's how the Zach Smiths came out. He's a rude, crude dude. Whether you use these or choose to improvise your own, I have a few pieces of advice: have fun, make it your own, be kind to your fellow cast mates...but also, yeah, mess with them. It's a thrilling scene to do, and I loved every second of it. Enjoy!

ZACH SMITH: Alright, turd tacos! I gotta say, I have had enough of this freakin' place. This school is disgusting! They do not properly maintain it. There was a lice outbreak, and they acted like we don't all put that talking hat on our heads our first year. Clean that thing out. Also, I was walking through the halls the other day, and saw a turd in the corner. A human turd. Some animal just dropped a deuce like this whole place is a public toilet. And, of course, the one non-magical dude who works here is the custodian. What's wrong with you people?! This. Place. Is. Gross! That's why I keep my stuff clean and protected. Even when I fool around, I stay safe. No mouth stuff, no direct inter-course. It's only over the pants stuff for old Zachy Smith. Alright, let's start these try-outs!

ZACH SMITH: Alright, butt butter pecan ice cream! Big news in my life. The other week I went scuba diving with my family. Everything was fine until a pygmy sperm whale bit me. I kicked it in the head and swam away. I didn't think much about it, until we got back to land, and they informed us that the area we were in was contaminated with radioactive animals. Then I thought of another butthole who was bitten by a radioactive animal, and what happened to him. I thought, "Let's do this." I got sick and woke up next day feeling great. I jumped in the ocean, and could swim like a damn fish. That's when I knew I had the powers of a pygmy sperm whale. Well, I looked them up, and realized I definitely did. What are their powers you ask? They release a brownish/red substance from their body to confuse animals. Basically, they shit themselves. That was my powers. I still decided to embrace them. So, I started small, and went to a public pool. I saw kids peeing in the pool, and said, "Stop your peeing, or feel the wrath of Pygmy Sperm Whale-Man!" They laughed, I made turds in the water, and I only made things worse, cause the public pool was now filled with my poo. Everybody laughed at me. So, I used my name. I got a costume to match the animal, all white, and went to the sea. I found criminals robbing a yacht, and swam up to them to stop them. I yelled, "It's me, Pygmy Sperm Whale-Man! I'm here to stop you!" They laughed at me, and said I just look like a sperm. So, I used my powers, made my poo, and nothing happened to the bad guys. I forgot I was the only one in the water, and was just swimming in my own feces. Finally, I heard a super villain was having a huge illegal toxic waste dumping ring. His name was King Starfish, and I went to face him. I went to announce myself. "I'm Pygmy Sperm Whale- Man, and he laughed at me. I challenged him to come fight me. He jumped in the water to fight. Once he did, I said, "Looks like you're shit out of luck." I pooped myself, he was consumed by it, and got a staph infection and died. And that's how Pygmy Sperm Whale-Man saved the world. Alright, let's start these try-outs!

ZACH SMITH: Listen up, sizzling fajita turds! I had a night last night. It was great! We visited the Prison of Ass-Cabin! I mented my aqua all over the place, if you know what I mean. Related topic: You know what I call my penis? The Phoenix! Cause one night with it, and you are reborn. Also, 'cause it burns when I pee! Alright let's start these try-outs!

Glossary of Puffs Words & Spells

Puffs Nouns (In seemingly no order)

A CERTAIN SCHOOL OF MAGIC & MAGIC: The name of the Wizard School the Puffs attend. You get it.

BRAVES: Just the best kids at the school.

SMARTS: These are kids who love books.

SNAKES: Ambitious. Cunning. Slithery. No legs. Scary.

SNAKES (HOUSE): A person who could make an adult cry.

PUFFS: Just the best kids at the something.

MUG BORNS: Those born of regular ol' Mugs, but can do the magics.

MAGIC: ...Really? You need us to define this? *Oh boy.*

DEATH BUDDIES: A group of friends 4 life, looking for good times, good memories. (Those good times being terrible and horrible things, don't be a Death Buddy.)

ADULT BUTTER BEVERAGE: A tasty drink to get butterbuzzed on, even if you are thirteen. (Butter responsibly.)

SOUL SUCKING SECURITY GUARDS: Underpaid and overworked nightmare fiends who are very good at their jobs except when they are not.

MAGIC: Again? Uh—it's the stuff that comes out of sticks? We good?

FLAVORED BEANS: There's lots of them.

SPORTS!!!!: This is the best we could do. It's the sports game. You know. The one everyone's always going on about, and everyone just happens to be really good at.

THE YULE-TIDE BALL: A special event which keeps you from going home for Christmas. AKA what you should certainly call any special event you do around the holidays in association with Puffs.

PIGSMEDE: This was the best I could do, okay?

MAGIC: The power of apparently influencing the course of events by using mysterious or supernatural forces.

Puffs Spells and What They Do

STUPIDFY: A spell for stunning.

OLIVE GARDIUM LEVIOSA: A spell for floating feathers, and *that's it.*

AVADA KEDABRA: A spell with a bright green light. (Really hit that –DABra")

ASIO: Brings things close to you, warning, you may get hit in face or drop books. (Pronounced Ah-sio.)

SNAKE SPELL: Summons Snaaaaakes!!

EAT SLUGS: Summons Sluuuuugs!!!

RICKMANSEMPRA: A scary spell for a brilliant man.

LOCOMOTOR LEGS: Make legs move. Like a…locomotor.

TARANTULA JELLY: Your guess is as good as mine.

The Publishers Wish to Thank:

Colin Waitt, Sarah Reynolds, and Charlie Crawford for formatting and assembling each edition; Heidi Tandy and Nathan Sheffield for helping us make it possible; Ed Iskandar, without whom none of us would have met; and all of the fans of *Puffs* who let us know how important this play has become to them.

Made in the USA
Middletown, DE
29 December 2018